EVERNHAM
Racer · Innovator · Leader

E V E R

Racer • Innovator • Leader

EVERNHAM
MOTORSPORTS™

TRIUMPH
BOOKS
CHICAGO

A TEHABI BOOK

N H A M

TRIUMPH BOOKS
CHICAGO

Distributed to the retail market by Triumph Books, 601 S. LaSalle St. Suite 500, Chicago, Illinois, 60605. Telephone: 312-939-3330; Fax: 312-663-3557.

Tehabi Books developed, designed, and produced *Evernham: Racer • Innovator • Leader,* and has conceived and produced many award-winning books that are recognized for their strong literary and visual content. Tehabi works with national and international publishers, corporations, institutions, and nonprofit groups to identify, develop, and implement comprehensive publishing programs. The name *Tehabi* is derived from a Hopi Indian legend and symbolizes the importance of teamwork. Tehabi Books is located in San Diego, California. www.tehabi.com

President Chris Capen
Senior Vice President Tom Lewis
Vice President, Development Andy Lewis
Editorial Director Nancy Cash
Director, Sales and Marketing Tim Connolly
Director, Corporate Publishing and Promotions Eric Pinkham
Director, Trade Relations Marty Remmell
Art Director Curt Boyer
Editor Terry Spohn
Author Deb Williams
Copy Editor Lisa Wolff
Proofreader Robin Witkin

Tehabi Books offers special discounts for bulk purchases for sales promotions and use as premiums. Specific, large quantity needs can be met with special editions, custom covers, and by repurposing existing materials. For more information, contact Eric Pinkham, Director of Corporate Publishing and Promotions, at Tehabi Books, 4920 Carroll Canyon Road, Suite 200, San Diego, California 92121-1725; or, by telephone, at 800-243-7259.

Photography credits appear on page 156.

Library of Congress Cataloging-in-Publication Data has been applied for.

First Edition

ISBN 1-57243-457-0 (trade hc)

Printed through Dai Nippon Printing Co., Ltd. in Hong Kong.

2 4 6 8 10 9 7 5 3 1

The paper used in this publication meets the minimum requirements of the American National Standard for Information Sciences—Permanence of Paper for Printed Library Materials, ANSI Z39.48-1984.

RACER, INNOVATOR, LEADER Ray Evernham ended his driving career in this D.I.R.T./Asphalt Modified, pages 6–7. He moved on to enjoy many successes like the one at Bristol, Tennessee, in March 1998, pages 8–9, as Jeff Gordon's crew chief. Now he continues his quest for racing excellence with his own team of two cars, including young Casey Atwood, pages 10–11, pitting during the 2001 Daytona 500 in Dodge's return to NASCAR racing. Seven-time NASCAR Winston Cup champion Dale Earnhardt, facing page, recognized that Ray's leadership and Jeff Gordon's driving ability made them the "team to beat" during the late 1990s.

RACER

INNOVATOR

LEADER

CONTENTS

FOREWORD

MY RELATIONSHIP WITH Ray Evernham began as a three-race Busch Series deal when we were young and trying to make it to the Winston Cup circuit. When it all began, we didn't even know each other, but we clicked immediately when it came to understanding the race car. I'd never had a crew chief when I competed in Sprint Cars and Midgets, let alone one who had driven race cars. So even though we didn't have a great deal in common away from the race track, we spoke the same language when it came to the cars. When racing was involved, everything came naturally.

Ray taught me a great deal about dedication because there's no one more committed than him. It's nice to have a person on your side who's that dedicated. His devotion to his job inspires those around him. You can see this dedication, not just in the long hours he puts in, or his continual self-improvement in all aspects of his job, but also in the way he listens to others, which is vital to good communication. When we were together, our communication was great—not because he could read my mind, but because he took the time to listen to what I had to say. If I told him the car was loose, together we broke down the corner and figured out where the problem existed. We figured everything out together, and learned from each other.

That quality is what makes Ray a leader. He values what everyone has to say, and that builds a team concept and motivates the members. He reads constantly and is very knowledgeable. He's a planner who thinks ahead and is prepared for anything that happens. And he's a good family man who loves his wife, Mary, and little Ray J. He would do anything for them. In spite of the fact that we compete against each other now, we're still friends, and we're always in the back of each other's minds.

FIND A WAY

IT'S 1978. A FEW MILES FROM ASBURY PARK, New Jersey, where local heroes Bruce Springsteen and the E Street Band rose to stardom

five years earlier, another local hero is trying to do the same thing—at 110 miles an hour. Locked in a pack of cars, deaf among

high-powered engines screaming through straight pipes, belted tightly into his driver's seat, defending Wall Stadium Modern Stock

champion "Hollywood" Ray Evernham is racing well tonight, just behind the leaders, his tires nicely scuffed by now as he slams

the pedal to the floor coming out of turn four and his car leaps back toward top speed. He checks to see who's behind, where the

squirrel in the yellow job is, and where that guy in the black Chevy behind him went.

There's a new vibration in Ray's shoulders now, something different, something just a little wrong, but there's no time for

that. At 110, just a little almost always means trouble, but you go until you win—or until something happens. Ray can feel that

guy behind making a move, coming high on him. Into the turn, Ray's head snaps forward as he hits the brakes, then pops back

against the seat as he comes out on the accelerator again, that different feeling up his right arm suddenly forgotten as the race

ahead disappears into a blanket of dust and tire smoke. One of the leaders has spun into the infield and back onto the track.

Somewhere in that cloud at least one car is blocking the track. Nowhere to go, no time to slow down, Ray drives blind right into it and suddenly out. Lucky again. Just as he checks for the yellow caution, the steering wheel pulls sharply to the right, yanked by a blown tire. In the split second before he hits the wall, with chunks of rubber hammering the wheel well, Ray pulls his hands from the steering wheel to save his thumbs.

Not the way he wanted to end his evening, but as he climbs out of the crumpled car Ray can feel no pain except the loss of a race. Even before both feet hit the ground he is assessing the visible damage to the car—snapped control arm, peeled sheet metal, bent frame, broken engine mounts—guessing whether they can repair it all in time for next week's race. He waves to the crowd to let them know he's okay. It will be a long week in the garage, but that's nothing new for Ray Evernham.

This is how it has always been: find Ray Evernham, and there'll be a car nearby. He might be in one, under one, or next to one. He might be sitting atop a transporter spotting for one during a race. He might be asleep, those precious few hours a night when he does sleep, and chances are he's dreaming of one. As a small boy in Hazlet, New Jersey, the most beloved toy he ever had wasn't a baseball mitt, football, or helmet. It wasn't even any of the dozens of Hot Wheels cars that seemed to scatter themselves daily across the floors of the Evernham home. It was a plastic Marxicart he could hop into and drive around the house. He was never interested in anything else. By the time he was old enough to nag his family into springing for something with a real motor—a go-kart—it was the backyard that absorbed the brunt of young Ray's passion.

Tagging along to the race track with his uncle Nick when he was eight years old gave Ray some pretty spectacular bragging rights at school, and yet, if you asked him, he couldn't tell you why he found racing so attractive. It may have been the speed. It may have been that a car was simply a machine, and he liked to work on things. All he knew as

FAST CARS Ray's high school car in 1975 was the 1968 Camaro SS at bottom. His second race car was a 1968 Camaro, right, that Ray showed off on senior prom night. He raced it at Wall Stadium that year.

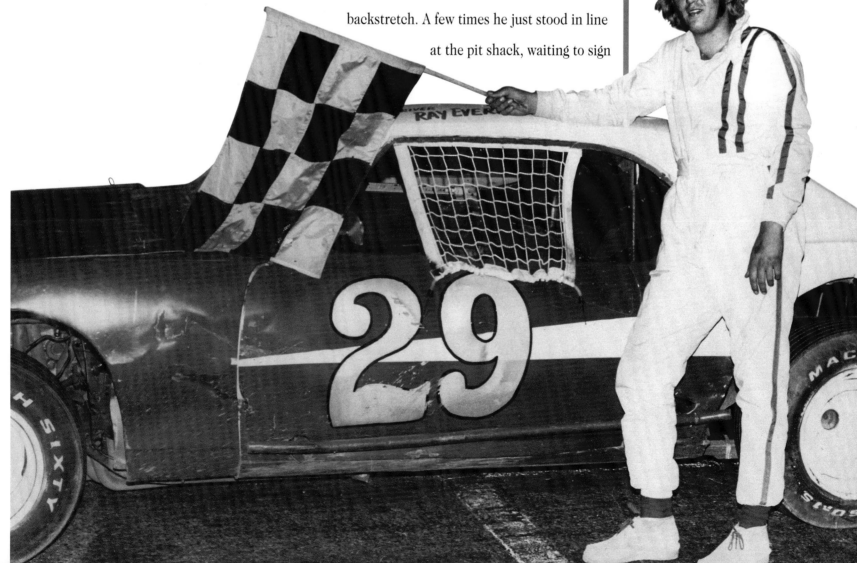

he approached his teenage years was that racing was not just something he wanted to do, it was a profession he was destined for. Long before he was old enough to drive legally on the streets, he was busy tearing up the backyard in his uncle Bobby's pickup truck, finishing the landscaping job he had started with the go-kart. It's not easy to keep a yard in the sandy clay of northern coastal New Jersey, and the Evernham backyard was a hopeless case. The grass had long since fled. Ruts and potholes were everywhere. Almost every summer day a plume of dust rose from that yard and settled in layers over the parked cars, porches, and mailboxes of the neighborhood.

When Ray turned seventeen and got his driver's license, he could drive to the races on his own, but there was still one legal obstacle. In New Jersey, no one under eighteen was allowed in the pits. For a determined young man like Ray, that really wasn't a problem, just another challenge. No one could keep him away from the half-mile dirt track at East Windsor, New Jersey, just east of Trenton. It was just a flat track with an unkempt grassy infield surrounded by bleachers made of wooden boards and cinder blocks, but to Ray it was the most gorgeous piece of turf in New Jersey. The concession stand sold great french fries, and sneaking in wasn't all that hard to do, since the pits were located outside the backstretch. A few times he just stood in line at the pit shack, waiting to sign

TASTE OF SUCCESS
Ray drove his Modern Stock Camaro to his first victory at Wall Stadium in 1976, en route to Rookie of the Year honors. Following spread: Ray (61) faced Jamie Tomaino (56) and Tony Hirshman (X9) many times in Modified races at Wall Stadium.

In the day we sweat it out in the streets
of a runaway American dream.
At night we ride through mansions of glory in
suicide machines.
—BRUCE SPRINGSTEEN

in, trying to look much older than he was. Most of the time, though, the easiest thing to do was climb into the cab of the truck they were using to tow the race car, hunker down in front of the passenger seat, and hide on the floorboards.

By the time he turned eighteen, Ray already had his own race car, with his brother, Willie, and longtime friend Shay Nappi. They built a Street Stock, or Modern Stock, as it was called then—a sweet little 1962 Nova with the Number 29 painted on the side. The teenagers could hardly contain their excitement. They were finally going to race, and the fact that they were going to do it on a paved track using tires suited for a dirt speedway seemed a minor detail. They flat-towed the car to Wall Stadium behind Nappi's personal car.

A third-mile asphalt paved track built in the 1950s, the Wall Stadium track sported 30-degree banked turns and concrete bleachers. It had been built in a gravel pit, so in order to race, competitors had to drive down below ground level to get to the track. The pit lane was above the track on the outside, next to the backstretch. Pitting during a race just wasn't practical. In order to reach the pits, a driver had to go out a gate on the backstretch and drive up a hill. Just getting there would cost two laps during a race. Wall Stadium soon became a familiar place to Ray, and he became a minor celebrity there. He competed in only a couple of events in 1975, but the following year he won rookie honors in the Modern Stock division. Then, in 1977, in only his second full season, he emerged as the Wall Stadium champion, adding eleven victories to his résumé. And it was while racing at Wall Stadium that Ray would begin a partnership to last a lifetime.

On one race day in September of 1977, Ray and other drivers made their way through the grandstand between events, helmets in hand, collecting funds for a fellow racer who had been injured.

Ray was then spending his free time with a group of young men known as the Bayshore Gang. Walt Rogers was considered the group's leader, since he was winning races and championships. The Bayshore Gang members were about ten years older than Ray, and a young woman named Mary Dowens lived a little way down the street from them. That September night, Mary had gone with the Rogers family to Wall Stadium to watch the races. When Gary Rogers and Ray sauntered into the grandstands, they both headed for the area where the Bayshore Gang was seated. Mary caught Ray's eye in the crowd and he headed in her direction. After all, he was a very cool, very popular race car driver nicknamed "Hollywood."

FAST TIMES

Ray drove his Camaro, top left, to the Modern Stock championship at Wall Stadium in 1977. Whether racing Modern Stock, Sportsman, or Modified cars, or relaxing on his dirt bike, bottom, "Hollywood" Ray was never far from an engine or from the hearts of fans like young Jamie Steger, facing page.

Racing in the Blood

RAY EVERNHAM SR., who enjoyed riding motorcycles, was quite an athlete, having played semi professional football and baseball. Later he worked in a gas station while his wife, Mary Lou, was employed as a nurse. At first neither parent took their middle child's interest in racing seriously, even though he had begged persistently for a go-cart as a boy.

Ray Jr. was about seven years old when he first spotted the go-kart he wanted at the Englishtown, New Jersey, flea market where his grandmother had a booth. For three or four weeks Ray pleaded with his parents to buy it for him. Finally, they surrendered.

The family property consisted of slightly more than an acre, with the house sitting on one corner. Ray kept the field torn up, speeding around the terrain every day with his go-kart. Every once in a while the frame would break, and Dad would weld it back together. If a tire went flat, young Ray continued driving, undaunted. The boy and the go-kart became one over the hours they spent together engraving deep tire ruts in the family's yard. But even though Ray loved the machine, he didn't like to work on it, opting instead for his father to repair it. The strong work ethic Ray has today didn't become a part of his personality until

he was about twenty-four years old.

The go-kart lasted only two or three years before Ray's uncle Bobby, who lived next door, gave him a pickup truck. Now, at ten years old, Ray began in earnest to redesign his parents' yard as he raced the truck around it.

Despite the hours he spent driving around the yard in various vehicles, it wasn't until Ray quit sports after his freshman year in high school that his parents realized he was serious about racing.

Soon afterward, they took a second mortgage on their house to erect a garage where he could build his race cars. His brother, Willie, worked with him. The boys' sister, Luann, was left to sacrifice many of the things she wanted because the family budget could go only so far.

With the exception of Luann, everyone else in the family has followed Ray south and into racing. His father handles maintenance for MB2 Motorsports, which fields Pontiacs for Ken Schrader, while Willie is a mechanic at Chip Ganassi Racing, where veteran Sterling Marlin drove the first Dodge to Victory Lane in 2001 in the Pepsi 400 at Brooklyn, Michigan.

FAMILY TIME
Ray and wife, Mary, celebrated the 1998 Winston Cup championship with Ray's parents, Mary Lou and Ray Sr., at the Waldorf-Astoria Hotel in New York City, center. It was Ray's last title as a crew chief. Ray's sister, Luann, with young Ray in their Sunday clothes, left.

DREAM REALIZED

Top: John Bauma (right) was half of the Bauma brothers, who gave Ray a Modified to race. Ray made his debut in the Bauma Modified at Wall Stadium a week after his twenty-first birthday. The Number 29 he drove at New Jersey New Egypt Speedway in 1980, bottom, was one of seven asphalt Modifieds Ray raced during his career.

After the races, spectators usually left the grandstand to go into the pits. When Mary showed up, Ray decided right then to learn whatever he could about the striking young woman. He invited her to a party at his house the next day. "There was just something about his whole body language," Mary would say years later. "Once I got to know him, I immediately felt that drive. It was something that just stuck out in his personality."

Mary drove her mother's car to Ray's parents' house that evening, where she encountered the usual Evernham scene: young men in their late teens ripping the yard apart racing motorcycles and cars. The yard looked like a junkyard. Rutted and potholed, it was crowded with cars and motorcycles of all kinds. Leery of the motorcycles careening around, Mary pulled into the front yard and her car immediately sank into the sand. Within moments, much to Mary's embarrassment, the partygoers had emptied out of the house to help dig her car free.

It was her welcome into the racing community, and it has been Ray and Mary ever since. They dated for six years before they became engaged and four years later were married. If you ask them today why it took so long, you'll get two different answers, both of them probably right. Mary will say the lengthy courtship ensued because they wanted to do everything the way it's supposed to be done. Ray will say he just wasn't ready to get married for a long time.

During the decade they dated while Ray struggled with his racing career, Mary took care of him, taking him to dinner, to the movies, and to the clothing store. When they first met, "Hollywood" Ray Evernham was the promising young racer who seemingly could do no wrong on the track, even when he wrecked a car. In 1978, however, Ray got his first dose of racing reality. He had taken every dollar he could scrape together and built a Sportsman car. It was like a Modified but had smaller tires and a smaller engine. Ray had carefully and lovingly turned that pile of sheet metal and engine parts into a finely tuned racing machine. But in less time than it took to turn a lap in its first race, it was gone.

The fatal move came when Ray dove to the inside to pass a car in front of him. He pulled in front too soon and got clipped. That turned him head-on into the wooden fence, which exploded when his

> We are blind until we see that in the human plan nothing is worth making if it does not make the man.

IN THE MONEY

Ray's first-ever NASCAR check, for his finish in the point standings at New Egypt Speedway, didn't break $100.

ON TOP

With Mary in the background watching from the frontstretch fence at Wall Stadium, Ray showed off another checkered flag added to his collection, top. During his driving career, Ray (19) battled with some of the legends in Modified racing, such as Richie Evans (61), bottom, at New Egypt in 1978 in a car Ray owned. Previous spread: Ray escaped injury when he wrecked this car without window netting.

car slammed into it. The impact sent the car tumbling through the air among the flying boards. There was no window netting on the car, and as it cartwheeled from bumper to bumper, Ray's head and left shoulder flew outside of the machine. Finally, the car landed on its wheels and spun like a top. By the time it stopped spinning, Ray could see only smoke and steam. Somewhere on the periphery of his consciousness someone was poking him in the shoulder, asking repeatedly if he was all right. Before the young driver had even qualified his new creation, he had destroyed it. Once he collected himself, his only thought was to wonder how he was ever going to pay for the pile of sheet metal. Ray retreated to his trailer in the infield, sat on the back of it, and cried.

Ray, Willie, cousin Danny, and some friends eventually rebuilt the car and ran it ten times that year, the final time on Ray's twenty-first birthday. He won that night thanks in part to a special birthday gift from his family and friends: a set of tires. It was that birthday victory that sent Ray's career in the direction he'd dreamed of for years—the high-powered Modified division. The Bauma brothers, John and Jim, who fielded an entry regularly at Wall Stadium, liked what they had seen in the young, flamboyant driver. They decided to give him a chance, so just a week after celebrating his twenty-first birthday, Ray made his debut in a Modified at Wall Stadium. The Bauma brothers wanted someone to pilot their Modifieds who was exciting and aggressive. Ray fit the bill, but the other side of the coin was that they would have to deal with many wrecked race cars.

Ray thought he had it made. He had always vowed that one day he would drive Modifieds, and now he was getting paid to sling the high-powered cars around bullrings from Thompson, Connecticut, to Martinsville, Virginia. For Ray, it was one big party. He didn't take it as seriously as he should have. He didn't care to learn about how to make the car work and handle or even to how to race. Success is not a good teacher, and Ray believed he was a successful racer. He always thought that if he could get in the car and drive the wheels off,

FATEFUL DAY

Paul Radford, Richie Evans, Corkie Cookman, Mike McLaughlin, Tom Baldwin, George Summers, Ray, Tommy Commerford, and Satch Worley came to the green flag at Martinsville Speedway in the race that nearly cost Ray his life. Following spread: In 1982 Ray raced Tony Sesley's Dirt Modified at Bridgeport, New Jersey.

that would be good enough. His attitude changed, however, on Halloween, 1982, in Virginia when he nearly lost his life in a fiery crash on the backstretch at Martinsville Speedway.

NEVER *underestimate your competition.*

The Modifieds had invaded the quaint half-mile track in the southern Virginia hills for the Cardinal 500 Classic. For drivers and crews, it was a frustrating race day filled with tire problems. Soon after making a pit stop for tires and fuel, Ray's Modified blew a right rear tire and slammed into the backstretch wall. In the brief moment of silence just after the impact, he could hear the other cars roaring past him.

Tony Siscone was following another car so closely that he didn't see Ray's wrecked machine. When the car in front veered to the inside to avoid Ray, it was too late for Siscone to take evasive action and he slammed into the wrecked car at full racing speed. The impact blew the roof off Ray's car and ripped its fuel cell apart. Fuel splashed into the air and the grandstand, then showered down on both of the cars as well as on Ray's back and helmet. Both cars spun around and as they stopped, they exploded in a ball of fire.

The rush of flames stole Ray's breath and he couldn't see his hands to unbuckle his seat belts. He fumbled frantically with the lap belt while his shoulder harness burned away and the fire erased his window netting. The steering wheel and everything connected to it had been crushed down onto his legs, and he couldn't get the pins off the wheel to release it. He finally managed to get one of his hands up over the roll bar and pull himself out of the seat. His eyelids were burned when his helmet shield began to melt. "This is not supposed to happen," he thought. "I am not supposed to die in this car."

Ray finally escaped and ran blindly, thinking he was still running through fire. Someone grabbed him by his suit and used an extinguisher to put out the fire on his body. He suffered second-degree burns around his neck, on his back, and on one arm, even though he was wearing fire-retardant underwear and gloves in addition to his single-layer fire-retardant driver suit. Siscone, who had slipped his ill-fitting gloves off earlier in the race, was burned horribly on the hands.

BUILDING AND REBUILDING Ray worked on his race car in 1978 in a friend's garage, top. The NASCAR-legal Modified at bottom was the car Ray built in early 1982 before the Martinsville fire. Facing page: this was the car burned in the fire. It was never used again.

THERE ISN'T ANY major trick in preparing a race car, since it is a machine that responds to the laws of physics. There are two keys to remember when building an oval-track race car: keep the weight low, and keep it to the left (The offset chassis on the Modified below is not allowed in Winston Cup cars). The more weight that can be kept on the left side when a car goes through a corner, the lighter the right side will be, thus enabling the driver to go faster.

The Basic Science

FIERY ESCAPE

Disabled by a flat and a crash into the wall, Ray's Modified was hit by Tony Siscone and the two cars burst into flames. Ray's helmet shield melted, and his shoulder harness burned away. Ray climbed out over the roll bar and ran, his arm and shoulder still in flames. Siscone suffered severe burns on his hands. Both drivers were saved from more serious injuries by their fire retardant clothing and quick action taken by Jim Soucy with a fire extinguisher.

Be prepared to
control the things
you can control,
and don't let the
other stuff slow
you down.'
—RAY EVERNHAM

It was the first life-altering experience for the fun-loving young driver, and one that left him with a choice, since he had once again lost everything. He decided to go to work and never give up. This meant getting a real job, something he had never had, since he had always been racing. Ray had no money and nothing with which to build a new car. He scoured the newspaper and found an ad for a job as a car salesman. There were plenty of other jobs listed in that paper, but it's likely Ray never ran his eyes past the section headed "Automotive." He searched his closet for his best clothes, donned a high-collar shirt and a knit tie, located the Lincoln-Mercury dealership, and strolled in, determined to convince owner Charlie Straub that he could sell cars.

Ray kept the job for six months, just long enough to save the money he needed to build another Modified. Once the car was built, he quit his job and turned his attention to racing again. But for the season's first three weeks he just couldn't get that car to handle right. Some people said he was scared because of the fiery crash at Martinsville, but Ray didn't believe that, and he hoped to put the accident—and all his competitors—behind him as quickly as he could. Thanks to another accident, Ray discovered the real source of his problem. When he had the wrecked car towed to the frame jig for a new snout, he found that the manufacturer hadn't properly built the frame, and the right side was an inch shorter than

the left. Buoyed by his discovery, he leaped into action. He repaired the car and won a race the next night.

Things were looking up, even though he missed winning the Modified championship at Wall Stadium by just twelve points. But the germ of an idea was beginning to stir, and it was a thought that Ray Evernham didn't want to consider. He turned away from it and back to racing with supreme confidence that he was a winning driver who was on his way up.

WINNING WAYS

Facing page: Ray began his racing career in Wall Stadium's Street Stock division, winning his first heat race in 1975 in a 1962 Chevrolet Nova. That's Ray out front, running dirt tires on an asphalt track. Five years later, he qualified this car at 139 mph at Trenton, New Jersey, Speedway in 1980.

On Track for Trouble

RAILROAD MAN

Every job Ray took had something to do with engines. The diesel he ran on the Port Jersey Railroad may have been the most powerful—and slowest—of them all.

RACING, EVEN small-time racing at the Jersey dirt tracks, was an expensive proposition. It could eat up all your money in the time it takes to wreck a car, or it could drain you dry over months of uneven finishes. Ray took on many jobs in his early racing days to make enough money to keep driving. Once, through his uncle Bob, the manager at the Port Jersey Railroad, Ray became an engineer. He worked the second shift on the short-line railroad because he could finish early and spend more time working on his race car. The job was fairly simple on paper: take the boxcars from Conrail and distribute them to the warehouses. Then collect them and move them back to Conrail.

One day Ray was extremely anxious to get off early. There was a race at Atlantic City Speedway the next day, and he needed to go home and spend time on his race car. His father was manning the controls that night, and they were running late. Although speed was important on the race track, caution was the only way to get there fast on the railroad tracks. Running a train too fast could cause it to pick a switch, which meant the wheels would go between the switch rails and jump tracks.

The route was only six miles long, but it was in the middle of Jersey City. Ray kept motioning his father to push the train faster. Finally, the heavy train reached its limit, jumped the track, and plowed down into the middle of the road. Ray jumped from the train, rolled on the ground, and then watched as the engine rumbled under a traffic light with the inertia of the boxcars behind pushing it. The wreck blocked the road. In no time, traffic lined up on either side of the locomotive, and horns began to honk impatiently. Ray walked off to make the dreaded phone call to his uncle.

"Uncle Bob, we derailed the train," he reported calmly.

"Oh. Can you get it back on?" Bob asked.

"Not this time."

"Where is it?"

"Where is it?" Ray took a deep breath, sighed, and said, "In the middle of Port Jersey Boulevard."

There would be no work on a race car that night. Ray had to stay with the train until a crane arrived to put the locomotive and cars back on the track.

He called Mary, who arrived in Jersey City with a small television, and the two sat in the caboose and watched TV until early morning. With the sun peeking over the Jersey shore and still no sight of the crane, Ray decided he could wait no longer. He had to get home so he could load up his race car and head for Atlantic City.

Ray reached the track in time to race, but his luck failed to improve. Another car broadsided him and destroyed his car. In that moment, Ray Evernham had become perhaps the only person in history to wreck a train and a race car in the same twenty-four-hour period.

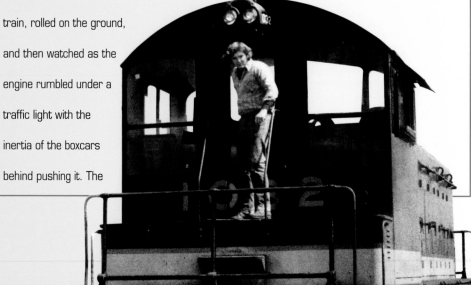

Ray lived on the Jersey shore, a good place for parties. His primary focus during the week was just that—partying. Racing became a weekend activity. He had advanced too fast in his driving career without paying enough dues. Ray had been able to acquire rides and sponsors fairly easily. He never thought about his physical condition and committed little time to working on the car. He partied all week while other people prepared his car. On Friday, the sunburned driver would come home and race. By that time the six-foot-one Ray, who weighed 130 pounds as a high school freshman, had ballooned to 215 pounds and sported long hair and a beard. Certainly he was a heartthrob to many young female racing fans, but the driver's seat seemed more cramped every time he climbed into the car.

The week leading into the Garden State Classic, one of the biggest races in New Jersey, was one long party at the shore. Ray was the favorite to win the race. He won the pole and led the first 150 laps, but his weight and his poor physical condition left him exhausted. Ray faded in the closing laps and had to settle for a top-five finish rather than a win. It was a heartbreaking experience. Ray had two choices. One was to stick his head under the covers and cry; the other was to fight harder. Needless to say, he chose the latter.

Twice he had worked his way back from being broke and built a winning car, so now there was no denying that persistent whisper in the back of his mind: the weak link in his racing career was Ray Evernham. People had loaned him money, kept their faith in him, and worked night and day by his side. But if his driving didn't cut it, the bottom line was that they couldn't win. Ray decided to begin a grueling workout program and stick to a healthy diet. He soon lost forty pounds and, with it, his cocky attitude. He decided the time had come to step up his career.

LATER DAYS

Ray in 1991, top, found his career looking up shortly before he suffered the head injury that ended his driving career. He piloted this Bauma-owned car in Pocono Raceway's Race of Champions, bottom.

TODAY, THE MAIN Evernham Motorsports garage sits in the lush green countryside outside Statesville, North Carolina, about fifty miles north of Charlotte. Inside, it is a beehive of activity where mechanics dressed in red and black work with a calm sense of urgency. Around the 40,000-square-foot shop sit more than a dozen race cars in various stages of assembly. These are the cars of the Dodge factory racing team being built from the floor up for upcoming races for each of the team's two drivers. In one area of the garage two semitrailers, the transporters, are being unloaded. Two race cars come out of their storage lofts in each trailer. Racing and qualifying engines, eight or more, sit lined up on their carts for shipment back to the engine shop. The job of cleaning, organizing, and inventorying everything on the trailer is called "turning around the truck." The transporter drivers do this after each race, working from a lengthy checklist.

WORK *in the same manner you expect your people to work.*

Upstairs, one of the pit crews reviews videotape of pit stops during the most recent race and discusses their times, their good points and weak ones, and ways to improve. They compare their work to that of competing crews on tape as well. They sit with their backs to the gym, a smallish room packed with bodybuilding equipment. The weight room would seem cramped

HIS OWN MAN

In close communication with his drivers, Ray studies the performance of his cars intently during practice and qualifying runs in the days before a race, constantly taking notes.

if it weren't for the mirrored walls on two sides; but even when working out, the crew members work together, spotting for one another while laughing and teasing.

Out in back of the building, the familiar growl of a Winston Cup racing engine roars out over the fields and a bright red Dodge race car rumbles to a halt along a low wooden wall, where Casey Atwood's pit crew leaps into action. It's practice time, and their goal is to change two right-side tires and refuel in fewer than six seconds. They work the same routine over and over, backing the car down to the far end of the pavement and racing it up to the marks each time just the way it will be done on pit road the next weekend in Pocono, Pennsylvania, or Talladega, Alabama, or Fontana, California. They are timing

STRENGTH TRAINING

First pioneered by Ray Evernham with the Rainbow Warriors, physical fitness training is a part of the preparation for success practiced by the Dew Crew, Casey Atwood's pit crew, here in the Evernham Motorsports facility.

*Teamwork is something
that I live my life by.*
—RAY EVERNHAM

TEAMWORK

Split-second timing wins races, and every last step a pit crewman takes during a pit stop is practiced many times. Facing page: Casey Atwood's Dew Crew pit team worked against the clock during the week before the 2001 Kmart 400 in Michigan on the practice pit behind the Evernham Motorsports garage. Bill Elliott's Dodge, left, got a quick turn in the pits at the 2001 Daytona 500, where he finished fifth.

themselves today, working up a good sweat in the 85-degree heat, but no one backs away from the

effort. The car roars to a stop and the tire men, the gun men, the jack man, and the gas man work with

an economy of effort that comes only from hours of drill and experience together. Tires roll away; the

car is dropped; and they've done it: gas and two new tires in 5.23 seconds.

Now they begin again; this time it will be a four-tire change. The car backs

away from the mark. The sun blazes through a steamy Carolina summer

afternoon. Locusts are screeching in the distance. The crewmen take their

positions along the wall, looking as one toward the car as it begins its run at them one more time.

BE WILLING to change direction when it is needed.

There are more than a hundred such racing hearts on the Evernham team. They are welders,

painters, shop foremen, pit crew members, engine mechanics, body men, race car drivers, and trans-

port drivers. The cars, the numbers 9 and 19 cars, are just the tip of this iceberg. A modern racing team

lives mostly out of sight of its fans but squarely in the headlights of its sponsors.

As a modern NASCAR racing team owner, Ray has much more to do than simply coordinate and lead

the activities of his crewmen and drivers. In the lobby of his garage outside Statesville there is a life-size

cardboard stand-up of Ray in his trademark black pants and red Dodge shirt, holding out a bottle of

Mountain Dew. Behind that poster stands a lot of work. Ray has to create and cultivate relationships with his

sponsors because they are the ones who pay most of the bills. Evernham Motorsports is one of

several Dodge racing teams, but they are the only Dodge factory team, and

as such they have a special relationship with Dodge.

Mountain Dew is one of the sponsors of Casey Atwood's car, and there are a number of other sponsors involved in the whole operation, including Ingersoll-Rand, Club Car, MAC Tools, Stihl, UAW-National Training Center, Valvoline, and Clausing.

Each time a major sponsor's rep visits Evernham Motorsports, Ray's schedule probably requires a change of shirts. His calendar may include half a dozen or more shirt changes during the week. Ray's closet at home is crammed with them, each bearing the sponsor's logo on one side of the front, "Evernham Motorsports" on the other. On top of that, there are often camera crews in the shop, or a photo crew, shooting for a feature or a television program or a print ad, and sometimes each of these shoots involves a handful of shirt changes. Visitors to the shop may enter the lobby to see Ray shooting a commercial or part of an upcoming television show, speaking from a script he has studied on the run earlier that morning.

When there are no television or photo shoots in the lobby of the Evernham Motorsports facility, visitors can roam around and look at the two red Dodge Intrepid R/T race cars, one each for the team's two Winston Cup drivers. There is a third car between them, a white Modified from the early 1990s; the last car "Hollywood" Ray Evernham drove in a race. You could say that Ray got from those backyard ruts in Hazlet to the Modified races at Wall Stadium to the backstretch battles on the superspeedways and the NASCAR Winston Cup championships to this modern shop by driving himself there. You wouldn't be wrong, but it never was quite that simple.

1. TEAM BEFORE INDIVIDUAL
2. DISCUSSION BEFORE CHANGE
3. QUESTION BEFORE MISTAKE
4. EFFORT BEFORE RESULTS
5. SMALL STEPS BEFORE GREAT DISTANCE

RIDING IN STYLE

Ray's first race car, the No. 29 Nova, went to its inaugural race towed behind Shay Nappi's personal car. Now his team's Dodge Intrepids travel to and from the tracks in two fully equipped transporters. Following spread: Enshrined between the team's two race cars at Evernham Motorsports is the last Modified Ray drove.

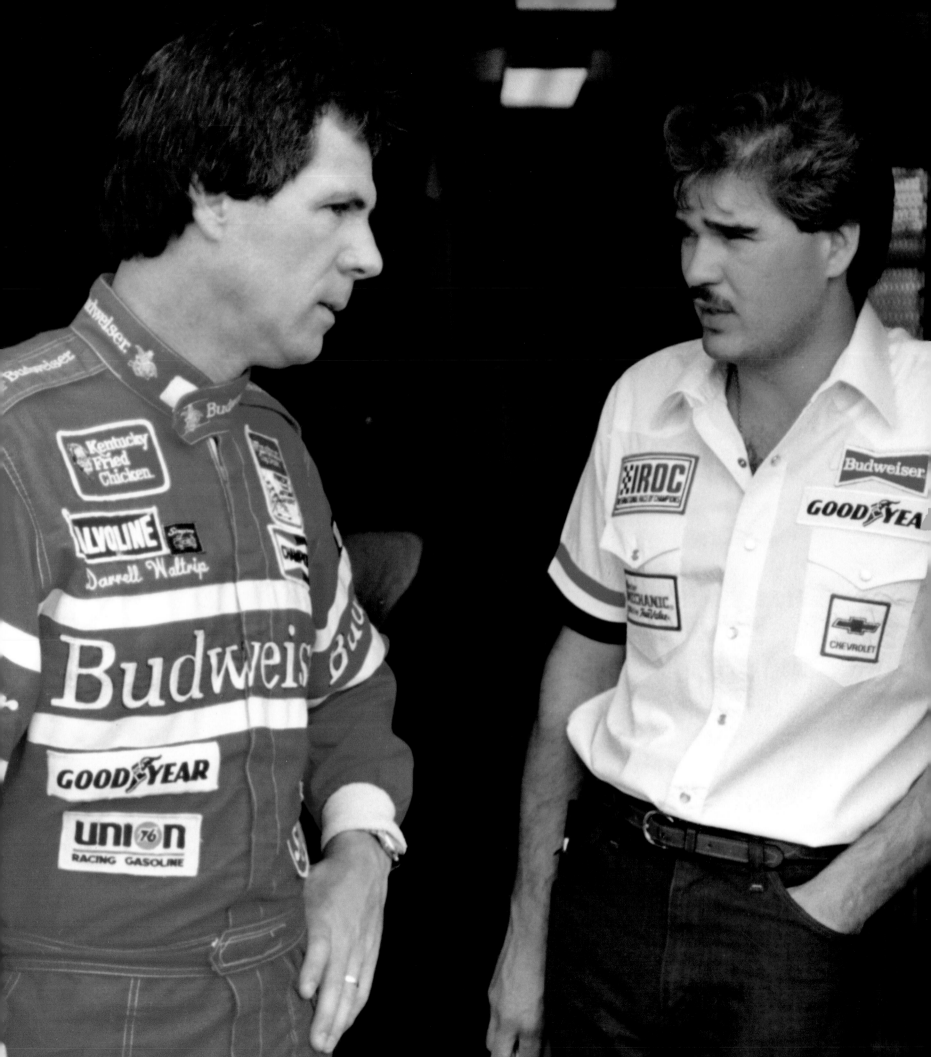

TURNING POINTS

HE HAD BEEN RACING for eight years, not counting the countless laps around his parents' yard as a child. He had driven almost every kind of car raced in New Jersey and won with most of them. He had also wrecked just about every car he had driven more than once and, despite his popularity and reputation, was living hand-to-mouth like most of the rest of the racers he knew. But Ray Evernham sensed he was close to making it in the big time, and he believed that all it would take to open the door for him was the right break from the right person.

In 1983, Ray decided to take a job with Jay Signore and his IROC program while he continued to race Modifieds. IROC—International Race of Champions—was a racing series that pitted the best drivers from all the major racing circuits against one another. The series, reborn after a three-year absence, featured top drivers from NASCAR, CART, IMSA, and Formula 1. They were given identically equipped and tuned cars, set up by a single team of elite mechanics, and pitted against one another in four races on a variety of tracks that would determine the best driver in the world. Ray figured he had finally gotten his act together. Everybody had picked him as the favorite to win the championship at Wall Stadium. He was now a hotshot Modified

. . . His passion and dedication separated him from the pack. It's just like they say, The cream always rises to the top.

—JAY SIGNORE

driver—one who concentrated on his cars, had become a good car builder, had gotten himself into good physical condition, and wasn't wearing himself out partying anymore. He was beginning to mature, and he was in demand among the car owners.

Ray's plan was to work for Roger Penske, who would then get to know him and realize what a good driver he was and inevitably decide to put him behind the wheel of one of his Indy cars. So Ray walked into the IROC program with what he thought was a foolproof plan for reaching the Indianapolis 500. From December 1983 until February 1989, his learning curve was steep. He test-drove IROC cars and met great drivers from around the world. He learned how to organize a workload and how to work with groups of people. From the standpoint of organizing a shop, Signore became Ray's greatest mentor.

Signore had worked with many mechanics and crew chiefs, but none of the others could claim responsibility for the large amount of gray in his dark hair. That distinction belonged to Ray Evernham. Ray's know-it-all-already attitude tested Signore's patience and good-natured character many times as he tried to teach Ray how to organize his workload and how to practice the delicate art of working with people. Sometimes Ray's interpretation of Signore's instructions left the IROC director shaking his head in disbelief.

Once, when IROC was scheduled to appear at Michigan International Speedway, the cars were having camshaft problems. Three days before the race none of the cars had engines in them. That's when Jay walked into the shop and gave Ray his instructions.

"Now, Ray," Signore said, "the motors are coming back, so make sure you organize all the parts so they're ready to go."

And that's exactly what Ray did. He organized the parts, not according to car and engine, but in piles. In one corner of the shop lay a pile of fan blades; in another, a pile of starters; yet another held a pile of carburetors. Each part had its own pile. Rather than creating a kit for each car, Ray had laid out a smorgasbord of parts.

In spite of this, Signore never micromanaged Ray, and the young mechanic gained confidence with each race. Over time, he mastered the process. In 1988 he invented the front side spoiler for the IROC-Z Camaros to use at Daytona. This simple device enabled the cars to remain closer to one another in the draft.

The experience at IROC was much more fruitful than it seemed at the time to Ray, who still itched to move his driving career forward. He was finally getting an education, but this school was about prepping race cars identically so the competitors would be driving cars that were as equally prepared as humanly possible. It was an assembly-line method of building race cars, taking identical parts and pieces and remaining absolutely consistent in tuning the engines. It may have seemed dull, but this drill was a lesson that would prove beneficial when Ray finally assumed the role of crew chief and eventually team owner in NASCAR. The ability to organize on a large scale, coupled with the other skills he acquired, gave Ray an edge. Since he had such a well-organized shop once he reached Winston Cup, more work could be completed in less time. That gave his team extra time to work on increasing their car's speed.

Ray met the best race car drivers in the world during the years he spent at IROC—legendary performers like Dale Earnhardt, A. J. Foyt, Mario Andretti, Tom Sneva, Darrell Waltrip, Neil Bonnett, and Danny Ongais.

CONNECTIONS

During his IROC days, Ray worked with top drivers from all of the major racing circuits. In 1989, they included Bill Elliott, Dale Earnhardt, Al Unser and Al Unser Jr., Terry Labonte, Al Holbert, Scott Pruett, and Geoff Bodine.

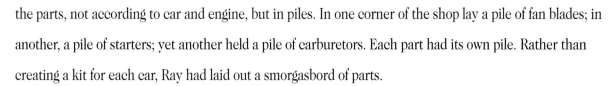

None of us is as smart as all of us.

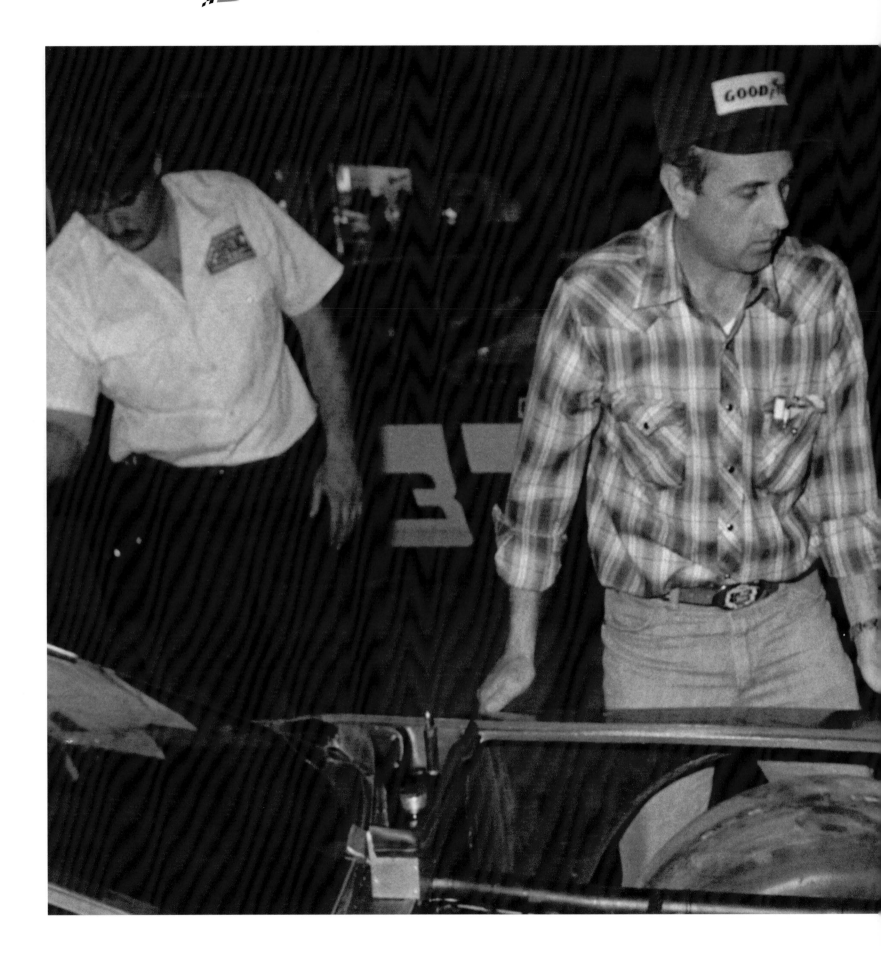

IROC RETURNS

From left, Ray, Dave Marcis, and Jay Signore at Daytona International Speedway in 1983, shaking down the first IROC car before the series returned after being dormant for three years.

He learned from watching them, listening to them describe how their cars were running, and then working to make their cars perform the way they desired. He was becoming a master racing mechanic.

But all through his IROC years, Ray still saw himself back behind the wheel in the future. Once, Roger Penske told Ray he would field an ARCA car for him. Another time it was an ASA car and he would be Rusty Wallace's teammate. Those deals never happened, and after six years the chance to drive Penske's Indy car seemed even further from possibility than when Ray had begun working there. Finally, he realized that Roger Penske was probably just too busy with his own career as a racing owner to have time to help Ray Evernham realize his own dreams. In 1989, Ray decided to leave IROC and return to racing full-time.

ON THE RIGHT PATH
Ray credits Jay Signore, top (right), with getting him headed in the right direction and teaching him how to organize a race shop. Driving the car at bottom, Ray nearly won the track championship at Wall Stadium in 1983. He lost the title by just twelve points.

It took him all of 1990 to build his own business—one that fielded Australian Dick Johnson's Winston Cup cars, while also maintaining two Modifieds, one for dirt and one for asphalt, and a Midget for Ray to drive. When the 1991 season arrived, Ray envisioned spending most of it behind the wheel of a race car. He had a new dirt-asphalt Modified, the Bauma Farms Number 19 NASCAR Modified, a Midget, and one of the Red Kote steel-tube cars left over from the effort with Johnson the previous year, which he planned to drive in ARCA.

Once again he began driving at Wall Stadium, setting a track record on the newly paved third-mile oval and easily winning the event. The following week a new track in Flemington, New Jersey, opened, and Ray ran second to Doug Hoffman in his debut there. The next day he was in Nazareth, Pennsylvania, and was leading when his car lost a cylinder and he had to settle for sixth. By the time the Memorial Day weekend arrived, he had won at Wall Stadium and had several top-five finishes at Flemington. He also had won some races with the Midget.

ONE SNOWY WINTER NIGHT, Ray, Willie, and Mary squeezed into the cab of Ray's little Ford F-150 pickup truck and headed for the Evernham house. All the way down the highway there were concrete dividers. Ray liked to slide the truck sideways and grind the step bumper off the concrete, shooting sparks as he went. Sliding the truck around in the snow was a trick he enjoyed so much that he had developed a routine. He would speed up the hill in front of his parents' house, crank the truck sideways, stand on the gas pedal, and broadside it into the yard. This particular night, though,

things didn't go as planned. Ray lost control of the pickup, slid through the yard, and bashed the truck into a tree in his uncle Bob's yard next door.

But the three really didn't consider it a problem. None of them was hurt and it was 3 A.M., so they piled out of the truck and went to bed. The next morning, when Uncle Bob got up and looked outside he saw a set of angry gouges in the snow starting at the end of his driveway and leading across the lawn. At the end of it sat Ray's pickup truck, mashed into the tree. For Uncle Bob, it was not an unusual sight in the

neighborhood, and sights like this one almost always had to do with Ray.

During the decade Ray and Mary dated, Ray gradually began to settle down. There were fewer surprises in the yard—or in the ditch at the edge of the yard—around the Evernham house. Ray had found the one person who could keep him anchored to reality, even if only slightly at first. And Mary, who worked at a bank, was smart enough to recognize that Ray's reality was racing. She always supported him in his dream. Each birthday or Christmas present from Mary was something Ray could use on the race car. Everybody else in Ray's life, probably a bit wishfully, bought him shirts and ties, but Ray lived in a T-shirt and jeans during those years. Mary bought tires, wheels, and tools, things Ray called "good stuff." She supported

Ray when he wasn't working. She took him out to dinner and to the movies, and she understood his white-hot passion for racing.

Today, when Ray comes home with a red or black Evernham Motorsports shirt on a hanger sporting yet another new sponsor logo on it, Mary shakes her head and smiles, wondering how they are ever going to fit it into the closet upstairs that is already crammed with such shirts. She has seen her husband go from the fringes of stock car racing to the top of the NASCAR world. She no longer has to buy him dinners to make sure he eats enough or take him to movies because he has no money in his pocket, but she is still his anchor, the force that keeps him grounded, and, as she has been all these years, Ray's most constant sponsor.

SPECIAL TIMES
In 1991, Ray quickly became adept at refueling his infant son, Ray J, top. In their footloose days, bottom, Ray and Mary enjoyed Atlantic City, in 1979.

Cast in a Winning Role

In 1982, Ray was a typical short-track racer, spending as much time as possible in a race car. That added up to four nights a week—two in Modifieds and two in a Midget. Ray campaigned a black Midget at Pinbrook, New Jersey, and Dorney Park, Pennsylvania, and it was the color of that ill-handling race car that played a dangerous role in a frightening accident one night at Dorney Park.

The Midget always had a tendency to bicycle—to hook up and then pick up its wheels. One night, Ray had been battling the car throughout the race. Finally, the car bicycled, got up on its side, and he knew all he could do was hang on.

The car bounced on its side, then back onto its wheels, twisted, and blasted through the track's wooden fence, splashing splintered boards in the air. Everything on the front of the car, including the axle, was driven backward. Ray's knee shattered against the steering wheel. His chest also hit the wheel, snapping his sternum.

Ray was knocked out, and when he began to come to, he thought his teeth were gone. Since the car was black no one saw the accident, so it was several laps before the yellow flag came out. By the time help arrived, Ray's chest hurt so much that he didn't notice the pain in his knee. He refused to be taken to the hospital, choosing instead to return home. During the ride back to New Jersey, he insisted he was all right while he swallowed his terrible pain. The next morning Ray could hardly walk, so he headed for the hospital. When the doctor had finished listing his broken bones, the hard-headed young driver looked him in the eye and cut to the chase: "Does this mean I have to miss the race Saturday night?"

The doctor was furious. "This means you can't drive this car for six weeks," he snapped. Ray and his crew were devastated at first, but not defeated. By the second week, they had made a special cast so they could slide Ray down into the Modified and arrange him so he could work the pedal. Once they had raced the Modified this way, they devised a way to slide Ray down through the top of the Midget. It was a tight squeeze, but when he won a race in that car, his achievement made the papers.

His doctor, who had treated most of Ray's injuries, was livid when he read the article. He walked up to Ray's mother, who worked at the same hospital, threw the paper on a table in front of her, and snapped, "I'm glad to see Raymond waited six weeks before he got back in the race car!"

MORE PAIN

Ray wrecked this Ted Siez Midget at Dorney Park, Pennsylvania, in a bad crash that left him with a broken kneecap and sternum.

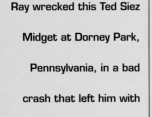

JUST KIDDING
At North Wilkesboro
Speedway, North Carolina,
in 1987, Dale Earnhardt,
top (center), posed with
Ray (right) and Jim Bauma.
Earnhardt had told Ray he
wasn't driving his car deep
enough into the turn. The
next thing Ray knew, he had
slammed the wall and
suffered a concussion.
When Earnhardt told him
he should have let off the
accelerator, Ray reminded
him of his earlier advice.
Earnhardt then admitted
he had only been kidding.
Ray and Mary, bottom,
waited together for his car
to be renumbered Number
20 for the Race of
Champions at Pocono,
Pennsylvania, in 1986.

It looked like the beginning of a big-time emergence for Ray, but the 1991 holiday weekend at Flemington was the beginning of the end of his driving career.

That night, Flemington had Triple 20s and Quadruple 20s on its racing card, events Ray hated because they consisted of simply running twenty laps with the hammer down. Flemington was a five-eighths-mile, fairly flat track that hosted dirt-asphalt cars that resembled Super Modifieds. These were cars with great big winged bodies that would average 135 miles per hour. In the first twenty-lap race, the fastest cars were relegated to the rear of the field because the lineup was determined by money earned, placing the high-point cars in back.

Mary was seven months pregnant by this time and was sitting in the first-turn grandstand when Ray's race began. The field managed only one lap before it got jumbled as they raced off the fourth turn. Ray hit the back of the car in front of him and got turned sideways. He quickly jerked the wheel to the right in an effort to save his car but got hit in the rear. That turned the car sideways again, and he shot across the track at about 100 miles per hour and slammed into the fourth-turn ambulance gate. The front wheels on Ray's car plowed through the gate, but the rear ones didn't. The impact was so severe that the car actually bounced back after it hit.

DIFFERENT DAYS

Ray spoke with open-wheel champion Rick Mears, top (left), before an IROC race at Watkins Glen, New York. After leaving IROC, bottom, Ray returned to Watkins Glen with his first Winston Cup car, driven by Dick Johnson. The crew, from left, were Ray's brother, Willie, Dan Stonemetz, Martin Piro, Ray, and Rick Guibard.

Mary, who had seen the whole thing, didn't think at first that the accident was severe. But then she realized her husband wasn't moving and saw the track crew rush to his aid. While she searched from her vantage point for some kind of movement inside the car, the crew waved for the ambulance, and Mary looked around to see track officials headed her way to take her to the local hospital with Ray. After two days he was transferred to the hospital in Red Bank, New Jersey.

Ray had suffered a severe concussion, and he drifted in and out of consciousness for a day and a half. During his conscious moments he was convinced he was fine. At one point, he telephoned the two men who worked at his race shop to tell them he was being held against his will. "Come pick me up; get the car ready," he said. "We're going to go race at Flemington this Saturday."

Much to his chagrin, no one came to get Ray out of his bed, and he spent nearly a week in the hospital. Once he was released, the effects of his injuries lingered. Dizzy spells kept him from working for a couple of weeks. Racing was forbidden until his doctor released him and he had passed a test under the scrutiny of Flemington's track officials. It took three months, the longest three months of Ray's life, to recover. He tried everything he could think of to hasten the process. He spent hours each day at a health club getting his body back into shape, and he

HITTING THE WALL
This impact marked the beginning of the end of Ray's driving career. Not long before Flemington's "soft wall" was installed, Ray had hit the old wall and suffered a serious closed head injury.

I assume I don't know anything, and it always keeps me very open-minded to learn.

—RAY EVERNHAM

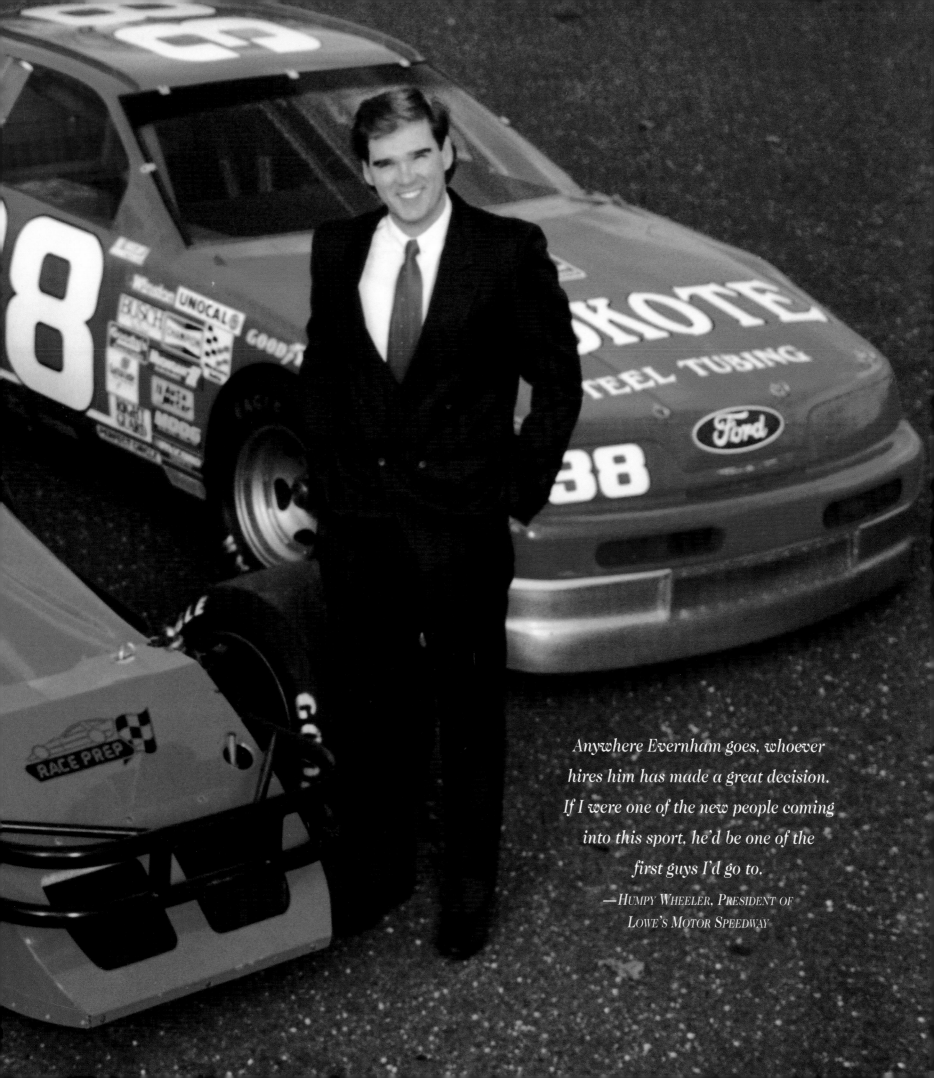

*Anywhere Evernham goes, whoever
hires him has made a great decision.
If I were one of the new people coming
into this sport, he'd be one of the
first guys I'd go to.*
—HUMPY WHEELER, PRESIDENT OF
LOWE'S MOTOR SPEEDWAY

discussed with various people the procedures he should follow to retrain his brain. He read more than he ever had, worked at depth perception exercises, and played video games in an effort to regain his dexterity and sharpness.

Driving wasn't the only prospect in Ray's future at that time. There were other possibilities calling, but they were calls Ray wasn't ready to answer. These calls were as persistent as the gnawing realization in the back of his mind that his driving career was taking him down a road that led nowhere. Whenever his telephone rang late at night in the middle of the 1991 season, Ray knew who was calling before he ever picked up the receiver. It was Alan Kulwicki, trying to entice him to move to North Carolina. But working for a low-budget NASCAR Winston Cup team whose driver was also its owner simply wasn't in Ray's plans. His time was consumed with rehabilitation, the kind that would hasten his return to the driver's cockpit.

When the day arrived for his test at Flemington, Ray discovered it would occur before more than just the track officials. NASCAR driver Ken Schrader was testing a Busch Series car that day, reeling off nineteen- and twenty-second laps on the five-eighths-mile track. When Schrader took a break, it was Ray's turn. He and some friends unloaded the Modified. It seemed as if it had been years since he had strapped on his helmet, but it felt good to be sliding behind the wheel once again. It was the first time he'd been in this particular car, but that didn't matter. He was comfortably back in familiar territory, and without hesitation ripped off a 16.50-second lap. When Ray pulled onto the pit road with a smile on his face, Schrader walked over and asked, "Isn't that the car that you just got hurt real bad in?"

"Yeah," Ray lied happily.

"How fast were you going?" Schrader asked.

"I think we ran a 16.50."

"Well, why don't you just take a gun and shoot yourself? It would be quicker," Schrader said.

Ray grinned and returned to the track, where he continued to click off one quick lap after another. In spite of the fact that he spun out once, he was cleared to return to racing. His scheduled comeback

> **Unless a man takes on more than he can possibly do, he will never do all he can do.**

NEW ERA

Previous spread: In preparation for the 1991 season, Ray had this promotional photo taken to use during his sponsorship hunt. Plans called for Ray to drive the Number 38 in an ARCA race at Pocono and the Number 19 in NASCAR Modified events, like the one at Wall Stadium, right. He also was scheduled to drive a Dirt Modified and participate in the Midget Series that year.

IT WAS A TYPICAL weekly race night at Wall Stadium, but on this evening one competitor was Tommy Baldwin Sr., whose son, Tommy Baldwin Jr., is now the crew chief for Ward Burton at Bill Davis Racing. Baldwin had ventured down from New England to test his skills against the New Jersey locals. In those days, each car's fire extinguisher was mounted on the sheet metal. During the feature event, Ray Evernham was headed for the front when his fire extinguisher came loose and began rolling around under his feet. When he accelerated, it rolled back under the seat. When Ray stepped on the brakes, it rolled forward again under his feet. Ray knew if he didn't get rid of it, the fire extinguisher might roll under the throttle and stick. It's hard to do much to solve a problem like that on a third-mile track with cars all around. Ray had to do something fast. He grabbed the fire extinguisher and tossed it out of his car, not realizing Baldwin was on his outside. The extinguisher hit the front of Baldwin's car and careened away.

At the end of the race, Baldwin came up and began shouting at Ray for throwing a fire extinguisher at him. Ray tried to explain, but it was no use—Baldwin walked away, shouting to all who could hear, "I'm never coming down to New Jersey and racing with these guys again. I'm passing a guy, and he throws a fire extinguisher at me."

Competitive Fire

TIGHT QUARTERS
Open-wheel Modified racing gets dicey if two drivers tangle wheels in a race. Here, Ray (19) duelled in close quarters with Tony Ciccone (51).

the next Saturday night at Flemington was rained out, and Ray, antsy as ever, couldn't sit still. He telephoned longtime friend Jim Bauma and asked if he could race his old Number 19 that night at Wall Stadium.

"Yeah. I ain't doing nothing with it. Come on and get it," Bauma told him. When Ray got there, he found the car hadn't been raced in months. It was covered in dust and the tires were flat. But Ray's desire to race that night wasn't dimmed by what he saw. He and Bauma threw the car onto the trailer and sped toward Wall Stadium, arriving just in time to make the last heat race. The lineup for the feature race showed Ray starting around twenty-fifth; but he finished fourth on his first night back, and that felt very good.

Things seemed to be back on track. Ray finally made his return at Flemington the following week and defeated Jimmy Horton in the feature. Everyone was happy and ticket sales were up, but Ray knew in his heart that things weren't quite right. He wasn't the driver he had been, though he was too proud to acknowledge it. The next week at Flemington, he had another serious accident. He was racing Kevin Collins side by side for a top-five position when they dove into turn three and a lapped car spun in front of them. The car was sitting sideways in Kevin's lane, but the driver, perhaps in panic, pulled his foot from the brake. His car rolled directly into Ray's path, and Ray slammed into the lapped car at 120 miles per hour.

He hit the car so hard his own car went up on its two front wheels and almost flipped over, then landed hard and went straight into the fence. Fortunately, Flemington had installed foam blocks around its outer barrier, and that was the only thing that saved Ray from another critical injury. However, the car's rear end still ripped out, and Ray's ankles took a severe beating when the driveshaft began flipping around. The hit was so hard that a knuckle on his hand popped out of joint and he had the wind knocked out of him. Ray was once again back on familiar ground—with another destroyed race car and more pain.

The wreck also aggravated an old injury. In 1982, Ray had broken his kneecap and sternum while driving the Midget. The sternum had never healed properly, so when his body took the hit that night at Flemington, it set him back another month. But he was a racer, and racers always come back, never thinking about the danger. It was nearly the end of the 1991 season when he made another comeback, this time at Thompson, Connecticut. His car ran well and Ray felt good.

Next on the schedule was a race at Nazareth, Pennsylvania, a prelude to the Indy car event. Roger Penske was there, and Ray was delighted to see him again. Ray and Doug Hoffman waged an

LOOKING AHEAD

In the early 1980s, Ray piloted this Midget, facing page, at the series home track in Pinebrook, New Jersey. Note the narrow shoulder harness. At this time, shoulder harnesses were not required to be three inches wide. When Ray got his job with IROC, his plan was to meet Roger Penske, bottom, and one day drive an open-wheel car for "The Captain."

READY TO GO

Ray was well prepared and eager for a Modified race at Nazareth, Pennsylvania. The 1991 race was a companion event for a CART race.

intense battle before Ray finally settled for second in the hundred-mile race. Immediately after the finish, Ray and his crew made a switch in the quick-change rear end and headed for Flemington. He never changed clothes, arriving at the short track still dressed in his driver's uniform. That night he got another second-place finish, this time to Kevin Collins.

He was now a guaranteed starter for the Flemington 200, but just before that race Ray got a call from an owner wanting him to drive a car he had driven years earlier in a NASCAR Modified race. He took the car out for practice before making a final decision. The machine felt pretty good in warm-ups, but on the heat race's first lap, Ray banged wheels with Ken Wooley and broke a tie rod. They repaired the car so Ray could race in the consolation event, which he won. That gained him a starting position in the rear of the field for the evening's feature race.

Within thirteen laps Ray was leading, having passed such Modified greats as Reggie Ruggerio, George Kent, and Jamie Tomaino. But then he slammed into the rear of a lapped car. He was tired, and his depth perception had become very poor when he was fatigued. He just couldn't judge distances the way he had been able to before his head injury. Worse, he couldn't tell ahead of time whether he was going to be good or bad. If Ray had won that night, it might have been a giant stepping-stone into a Busch Series or Winston Cup ride. But he knew more strongly than ever that he was having trouble.

Finally it was time for the Flemington 200, and Ray was intent on scuffing tires before the event. He was barreling down the front straightaway in his Super Dirt Modified at 135 miles per hour when the right front spindle broke. The wheel flew off and headed straight into the guardrail. This time the car hit the foam blocks so hard that it buried itself in them, with the rear wheels suspended in the air. Once again Ray had the wind knocked out of him and was slammed into the windshield, cutting open his chin. It took a forklift to haul the car back to the pits.

THE NUMBERS OF CARS RAY EVERNHAM HAS DRIVEN

No.   1   Midget
No.   2   Modified (Dirt/Asphalt)
No.   10   Midget
No.   15   Modified
No.   16   Modified (Dirt)
No.   19   Modified
No.   19   Sportsman
No.   28   Modified
No.   29   Modern Stock
No.   29   Modified
No.   56   Midget
No.   60   Modified (Dirt)
No.   61   Modified
No.   66   Modified
No.   74   Modified (Dirt)/
            Huffaker Fiero at Elkhart Lake
No. 201   Modified (Dirt)

DURING HIS DRIVING CAREER, RAY EVERNHAM EITHER TESTED OR RACED AT TWENTY-EIGHT TRACKS:

Daytona International
    Speedway, Fla.
Talladega
    Superspeedway, Ala.
Watkins Glen
    International, N.Y.
Riverside International
    Raceway, Calif.
Mid-Ohio
Michigan International
    Speedway
Wall Stadium, N.J.
New Egypt, N.J.
Flemington, N.J.
Trenton, N.J.
Bridgeport, N.J. (Dirt)
Syracuse, N.Y. (Dirt)

Thompson, Conn.
Westboro, Mass.
Cayuga, Canada
Martinsville, Va.
North Wilkesboro, N.C.
Pinebrook, N.J.
Freeport, N.Y.
Dorney Park, Pa.
Evergreen, Pa.
Pocono, Pa.
Elkhart Lake, Wis.
Lehigh Valley, Pa.
Atlantic City, N.J.
Loudon, N.H.
Talladega Short Track, Ala.
Shangri La (Owego), N.Y.

RAY EVERNHAM'S DRIVING RECORDS

- 1975 Modern Stock. 3 races.
- 1976 Modern Stock. 2 wins, Rookie of the Year, Wall Stadium.
- 1977 Modern Stock. 10 wins, Track Champion, Wall Stadium.
- 1978 Modified Sportsman, 10 races, 1 win; Modified, 5 races, 4 top 10 finishes;
  Full-time Modified, had his best point finish, second at Wall Stadium.
- 1979 Modified. NASCAR Rookie of the Year, New Egypt (N.J.) Speedway.
- 1982 Midget. 1 feature win. Broke kneecap and sternum in a Midget at Dorney Park, Pa. Modified. Burned in 2-car fiery crash at Martinsville (Va.) Speedway.

- 1983 Modified. 3 wins, 2nd in points at Wall Stadium.
- 1984–1989. Test driver for IROC.
- 1984–1990. Part-time driver while working full-time at IROC. Competed in as few as 1 and as many as 15 races annually. Won 3 races.
- 1991. Left IROC and returned to driving full-time. Had 1 win at Wall Stadium and 1 at Flemington, N.J., before suffering a closed head injury that ended his driving career.

ON EXHIBIT

This Dirt Modified now sits in the showroom at Evernham Motorsports.

Alan [Kulwicki]
was the smartest
man I ever met.
—Ray Evernham

Some time later on the same track, Ray found himself back in the pits after yet another collision with the wall during pre-race practice. With his crew shouting, "We can fix it," Ray replied, "Well I don't know who you're going to get to drive it." But his voice was lost in the frantic work to cut the snout off the car and weld it back. Ray climbed back in, took a five-lap warm-up, and agreed to start in the rear of the field. Ninety or so laps into the race, two cars tangled in front of him. Ray spun and hit them with the front wheels of his Modified, and his front axle exploded. Ray was finished. He unclipped his belts, walked away from the wreckage, and said, "Boys, I've had enough." He bid farewell to his driving career that night, packed his bags, and headed for North Carolina to take a job with Alan Kulwicki.

It had been a long time coming, and it came as no surprise to Mary, for whom it was a relief. She knew Ray had been having a problem. His temper was shorter, and sometimes he would just go off into the distance, even in the middle of a conversation. In her heart, even though she knew it was very tough on Ray, she was glad he had finally realized his driving days were over. Ray J had been born July 18, 1991, and there was more to be concerned with now than just the two of them.

It was a very angry thirty-four-year-old who packed his belongings and moved to North Carolina to join Kulwicki. Not only was Ray having difficulty dealing with the loss of his driving career, but things weren't going well financially, and he had no idea what was going to happen with the rest of his life. It seemed he was giving up his dream and settling for a consolation prize, and Ray was not prepared to accept less than success. When he arrived in January 1992 to join Kulwicki's operation, the shop was located behind the 1.5-mile track then known as Charlotte Motor Speedway. But Ray couldn't afford to live in the high-priced apartment complexes in Charlotte. He headed for Concord, about fifteen minutes northeast of the speedway, where he found an apartment that would meet his needs. It had only one bedroom, and the bed folded out of the wall, but his wife and their six-month-old baby were still living in New Jersey, so it didn't matter. Besides, it was only $350 a month.

Although Alan and Ray had good telephone discussions over the previous year about race car chassis and setups, their attempt to work together was not nearly as

WINSTON CUP

Alan Kulwicki, facing page and bottom (left), and Ray would often talk late at night on technical matters. Kulwicki finally convinced Ray to come work with him and crew chief Paul Andrews, bottom (right), at the beginning of the 1992 season. However, the relationship didn't last two months, and Ray left the team at Daytona soon after it arrived for Speedweeks that year.

SWEET AND BITTERSWEET
Bill Davis, Jeff Gordon, and
Ray celebrated victory at
Charlotte in May 1992, top
and facing page. Following
spread: Jeff Gordon (24),
with Ray as his crew chief,
duelled Alan Kulwicki (7) at
the start of the 1993
season. Kulwicki was killed
in a plane crash April 1.

congenial. It got off to a rocky start and degraded into a disaster. Ray thought he knew more than he did. In reality, he did know a great deal about race cars, but he knew nothing about Winston Cup racing.

This in itself isn't unusual—it happens to almost everyone who comes into Winston Cup from somewhere else. It takes a great deal of adjustment, and it was that adjustment period that was difficult for the headstrong Ray Evernham, who still hadn't completely come to terms with the fact that his driving career was over. They hadn't been together long before he and Kulwicki were throwing small items at each other in the shop and arguing constantly. Alan tried to teach Ray the way he wanted things done, but Ray wouldn't listen. The problem was simple: they were too much alike. Alan didn't have the patience to listen, either. And Ray couldn't understand why Alan wouldn't want to do something the right way, which was his way.

In just five weeks, the two men's stubbornness had wrecked their working relationship. Ray walked out of the Winston Cup garage at Daytona International Speedway at the beginning of Speedweeks 1992 with the intention of heading home to New Jersey. He now had no job, no money, and no prospect of driving again. It seemed he had failed at everything that he had set out to do. He walked toward the parking lot that day with no idea what he was going to do next. His life seemed to have reached a dead end. On the way to his car, he ran into a man named Preston Miller, who worked as the liaison between Ford Motor Company and its NASCAR Winston Cup and Busch Series teams. Preston casually asked him how he was doing and Ray told him the whole story. He was finished. He was going home. They talked briefly, and in that short time Preston, who knew a talent when he saw one, convinced Ray not to leave just yet. He suggested that Ray take the short walk over to the Busch Series garage to the Ford team fielded by Bill Davis. The Arkansas native had a young driver named Jeff Gordon, and he'd been looking for some help.

NASCAR Winston Cup Series
CHARLOTTE MOTOR SPEEDWAY
CHAMPION 300
NASCAR Winston
Baby Ruth
Ford
1

The Right Car for the Track

NASCAR WINSTON CUP races are run on three basic kinds of tracks—superspeedways like Talladega, Alabama, where the speeds are higher and engine horsepower is limited by restrictor plates for safety; short tracks like Bristol, Tennessee, where engines perform up to their full 750 hp but speeds are lower due to the tight turns; and road courses like Sears Point, California, that contain a variety of turns, as well as elevation changes. Racing teams build a different type of car for each track.

The speedway car is built to reduce drag as much as possible especially when engine power is cut to about 450 hp by restrictor plates at Daytona and Talladega, where maximum speed on the long straight-aways is vital. The body is mounted forward on the frame and is less contoured along the sides, and the grille opening is almost completely taped over to reduce the drag-producing airflow to the absolute minimum.

A downforce car is recognizable by its drag-producing elements. The body is mounted about 3 inches further back on the frame, and has more curvature in the front fenders to increase downforce, which helps hold the car to the track in the tight turns. Two extra mesh openings in the front of the body below the headlight locations allow cooling air onto the brakes, and often an extra hole is cut into the side window to vent more air onto the rear brakes. On a short track, the tighter turns and unrestricted engine power add up to more brake wear, and brakes would burn up quickly without the added airflow.

On a road course, the driver is called upon not only to make sharp right and left turns, but also to do a lot of shifting in the turns and upgrades. A car set up for this type of track is also usually built with fuel inlet holes on both sides of the body, to be prepared for the eventuality that it may be assigned to a right-side pit lane.

Cars are built to handle the biggest strain they'll encounter on each track. Anything could go wrong in a race, but generally on a super-speedway teams hope their engine holds out; on a short track they worry about the brakes; on a road course they watch both the transmission and the brakes.

DOWNFORCE CAR

Jeff Gordon (next to the driver's side window) and the Rainbow Warriors raced this car to a third place finish on the short track at Richmond International Raceway in the 1997 Exide 400.

Qualifying and Race Trim

WHEN A CAR is prepared for qualifying, the setup is quite different than it will be for race trim. For the qualifying run, it is actually set up to abuse the tires for one lap or two; in race trim, the goal is to save the tires. For the qualifying laps, the object is to put as much heat into the tires as quickly as possible to get more speed out of the car within the two laps allowed; in race trim, the object is to keep the heat out of the tires so they will last longer.

For the short qualifying run, the engine, oils, and gears are lighter. As close as Winston Cup qualifying is now, crews must look for any advantage to gain a hundredth of a second. At 200 miles per hour, a car travels 316 feet per second, so each second translates into the length of a football field on the track. A second cut off a pit stop, or a few hundredths of a second here and there in the car setup, can spell the difference between winning and losing. Crews take anything they can get. An ounce of weight, any little piece of horsepower, any kind of drag or downforce, a half-pound of air pressure— the small details can make the big difference in qualifying and earning a pole or starting back in the pack. To win the race itself, crews are still looking for that minute edge; but instead of setting up to last two laps, in race trim the car normally has to perform at top efficiency for five hundred miles.

SPEEDING TO TITLES
The multicolored Number 24 driven by Jeff Gordon and prepared under Ray's watchful eye became one of the most formidable entries in stock car racing history.

Ray has an amazing ability to get 100 percent of everyone around him, all these guys, including myself. I do think he's the best crew chief to come along in a long time. He's not only a great motivator and a coach, but he's also somebody I call a friend.

—JEFF GORDON

RAINBOW WARRIORS

WHEN RAY FOLLOWED Preston Miller into the crowded Busch Series garage at Daytona International Speedway, he didn't know what

he was walking into. He was sure of only one thing: he needed a job. The two men walked over to Bill Davis's race car, where Davis

was talking to a young driver named Jeff Gordon, the Busch circuit's top rookie for 1991. Ray and Jeff had worked together briefly

in a three-race Busch deal in 1990 and then went their separate ways. Davis's plans for Gordon, who was the USAC Silver Crown

champion and former USAC Midget titleholder, included one more year in the Busch Series and then an elevation to the Winston

Cup circuit. Since Ray had been a driver, he and Gordon spoke the same language fluently. Ray easily understood Jeff when he

explained his car's behavior on the track. By the end of the 1992 season, Gordon had captured a Busch Series record of eleven

poles and appeared headed for stardom. But it was a different story for Davis, whose future plans with Jeff began unraveling in

midseason when Winston Cup team owner Rick Hendrick stepped into the picture.

Hendrick had kept a watchful eye on Gordon ever since he had made his Busch Series debut. The Charlotte businessman

was astute at recognizing young talent, and he wanted Gordon to join his organization. Hendrick soon discovered that one of his

employees was Gordon's roommate. He called him into his office and asked him to talk to Gordon for him, to see if the young driver was interested in leaving Davis. Before midsummer, a direct meeting between Gordon and Hendrick was arranged. It was already public knowledge that Davis was without a sponsor for 1993, so as far as Hendrick was concerned, Gordon was a free agent. The meeting went well. The young driver had only one major demand: he wanted his current crew chief, Ray Evernham, to move with him.

For Jeff Gordon, not only did his professional relationship with Ray mark the first time he'd ever worked with someone who had driven a race car, it was the first time he'd even had a crew chief. The position didn't exist in Sprint Cars and Midgets.

Ray was open to the idea of moving to Hendrick Motorsports, but he didn't want to continue as Gordon's crew chief. He told Hendrick Motorsports Vice President Jimmy Johnson that he wanted to be the team manager. Johnson balked at the idea, but Ray was steadfast. He didn't think he was good enough to be a Winston Cup crew chief. In the end, Ray relented because it was the only way Johnson would hire him.

Ray resigned from Davis's organization in mid-1992 and moved his toolbox closer to Charlotte. Unlike many others who had found themselves in the same position, he began by evaluating himself and examining the definition of a crew chief. Aside from the technical expertise required, Ray came to the conclusion that a crew chief wasn't just an overseer of everyone's jobs; he was a coach. He decided he shouldn't just guide his employees; he should coach them. That meant finding a better way to relate to people and motivate them. He had to learn how to put in place some of the systems that he had learned without jamming them down people's throats. He had to get his people to believe in a project or a philosophy before he could expect them to follow it.

OUT FRONT

In 1992 in the Busch Series, top, Jeff Gordon's peers mainly saw his rear bumper, particularly at the start. That year Gordon won a record eleven poles. Bottom: At Atlanta in 1995, the Rainbow Warriors reached another goal on their checklist after their first Winston Cup championship.

TEAM #24 CHECKLIST

☑ From Nobody To Upstart

☑ From Upstart To Contender

☑ From Contender To Winner

☑ From Winner To Champion

From Champion To Dynasty

Ray had never liked school, and had never had good study habits, but now he thirsted for knowledge. He read books on topics ranging from philosophy to vehicle dynamics. Books by NBA coach Pat Riley, NFL coach Vince Lombardi, civil rights activist Martin Luther King Jr., and scientist Albert Einstein were his primary sources. It was from Riley's book, *The Winner Within,* that Ray borrowed the now-famous chart for success that hung on the wall just outside his office.

Several crewmen, including Ed Guzzo and Brian Whitesell, elected to leave Alan Kulwicki in the middle of his championship battle and follow Ray. Andy Papthanassiou also left Kulwicki to become Ray's pit crew coach, a newly created position that included duties as a fitness trainer—another of Ray's innovations that would soon pay major dividends. Ray worked with Andy on understanding pit stops. He traveled to wind tunnels and chassis shops. He called everyone he thought might give him even a thread of knowledge on tire and shock development. He even constructed a setup machine. At least one inspirational phrase could be found hanging on every wall in the shop, and the signs were changed regularly.

SHARE *your vision often, and soon your team will see it, too.*

THE FORCE

The Rainbow Warriors, below in 1993, adopted Ray's vision, working together to take the Hendrick Motorsports' operation to stock car racing's pinnacle. Following spread: The success began with the close connection Ray and Jeff Gordon (right) established in 1992.

I look to Ray more as a coach than a crew chief . . . Ray is a great leader. He is a man who can instill in others the desire to win.

—JEFF GORDON, 1993 WINSTON CUP ROOKIE OF THE YEAR

The team's debut in the 1992 season finale at Atlanta was hardly noticed, as it was the last race of Richard Petty's illustrious career and the climax of the closest point battle in NASCAR Winston Cup history, between Bill Elliott and Alan Kulwicki. But only three months later, Gordon would leave his mark on the Winston Cup landscape.

STRONG *belief in a project by its leader trickles down to the troops.*

SPEED WHILE STOPPED

Having a fast car was half the story. Ray's goal for the pit crew was to build a sense of teamwork that would inspire extra effort and creativity and help mold these individuals into a unit.

Ray's objectives for his team's first season were simple: win rookie honors and get the new Hendrick organization competitive. No one knew what to expect. It was a rookie team with a rookie driver and a rookie crew chief. Gordon's competitors for the rookie title were Bobby Labonte in Davis's car and Kenny Wallace in Felix Sabates's entry. All the team wanted was to learn and to do a good job. It was a stressful season; Gordon was involved in numerous accidents and tore up several cars. He had never driven in races as long as those on the Winston Cup circuit. Together, Ray and Jeff learned how to position the car's chassis setup at the beginning of a race, and how it was supposed to react during a lengthy green-flag run. At times they struggled, and there were days when Jeff's focus would drift and Ray would have to be the disciplinarian.

Still, throughout that educational year, the team accomplished much more than was expected, and at times there were glimpses of the brilliance that was to come.

When Ray had decided to hire Andy Papthanassiou as fitness coach, Jimmy Johnson didn't understand the relationship between weight training and crew performance. No other NASCAR crew had ever incorporated a physical fitness regime into their program, so they got no weight training equipment. Andy was forced to improvise. The team constructed a chin-up bar, and the men would carry one another on their backs to build strength and endurance. They ran with tires instead of weights. One of the signs they worked beneath quoted Muhammad Ali: "The battle is won in the gym, away from the lights and the crowds." Ray used that slogan to emphasize that a race had to be won in the shop, that all the team could do once it arrived at the track was lose it. Their work

paid off during the team's rookie season. They could travel to the track with a fifteenth-place car, but finish in the top ten because the pit crew produced a top-five performance. When most teams were turning in seventeen- to eighteen-second pit stops for four-tire changes, Ray's crew was in the mid-sixteen-second range. Once it became evident that Ray's approach to training the team's over-the-wall crew worked, they got their weight training equipment. By the time the crew reached the 1995 season, they were finely tuned and rarely surpassed.

With their arrival at Daytona in February 1993, the crew immediately turned heads in the motorsports community when Gordon won a Gatorade Twin 125-mile qualifying race. It was surprising enough that Gordon, at age twenty-one, had become the youngest driver in thirty years to claim one of the qualifying races. But when the other competitors saw the pit crew in the fields early in the morning going through their routine of stretching and calisthenics, many were dumbfounded.

The team was inconsistent but still managed to claim second in the longest race of the series—the Coca-Cola 600 at Charlotte—and earn the pole for Charlotte's October event, the Mello Yello 500. By this time, Gordon was more than a first-year driver; he was a rookie sensation and would soon be dubbed "The Kid" by veteran Dale Earnhardt, who was often referred to as "The Man." When the thirty-race season concluded on November 12 in Atlanta, Earnhardt had his sixth Winston Cup championship, Gordon owned the rookie title along with a fourteenth-place finish in the point standings. As for himself, Ray was certain that he didn't know as much as he had thought he did. The thirty-six-year-old crew chief stepped up his use of Hendrick's resources and increased his studies.

The team name, Rainbow Warriors, began to take shape sometime during that year. The rainbows on the firesuits and the color swatch on the car were distinctive, but no one identified the team with any name until a fan sent them a large photo of a Greenpeace boat named the *Rainbow Warrior.* The name seemed meant for them, especially since Ray already had begun his team-building process with a circular chair arrangement for meetings. Embracing the idea of being a tribe seemed to accelerate the sense that they were uniquely bonded, and the growing spirit seemed palpable. Ray gave out eagle feathers and promoted Native American tribal identity stressing bravery and courage to nurture that spirit.

FIRST POLE

The Mello Yello 500, October 10, 1993, was a strong showing for the young Number 24 team. Jeff Gordon won the pole and finished fifth in the race, which virtually assured him of Rookie of the Year honors.

Consistency, a point-race win, and a top-ten finish in the Winston Cup standings were the goals Ray set for his team's sophomore season. The cars had to improve, as did the pit stops. The engine program wasn't lacking, but Ray knew the organization's other two entries piloted by Terry Labonte and Ken Schrader were ahead of his in performance. That began changing in May 1994, at Charlotte. After Gordon wrecked in the Winston Select, Ray elected to rebuild the damaged car in three days rather than produce a new one for the Coca-Cola 600. Just four days after the all-star race, Gordon began his historic weekend in the rebuilt car by earning the pole position. In the waning stages of the race, Rusty Wallace looked as though he had successfully dispensed with Geoff Bodine and Ernie Irvan. But the race's complexion changed dramatically in the final seventy-seven laps.

One by one, the drivers on the lead lap made their final pit stop. Gordon remained on the track under Ray Evernham's watchful eye. The sophomore Winston Cup crew chief studied each adversary's pit stop. Wallace took four new tires when his Ford received fuel. It was then that Ray, watching the dramatic story unfold from atop the war wagon in the team's pit, made a decision that stunned everyone. His young driver would receive only two right-side tires when his Chevrolet took on fuel. Everyone, except Ray and his driver, felt it was a mistake. How could only two new tires beat four? It didn't make sense.

The quick stop returned Gordon to the track in second behind Ricky Rudd, who was trying to go the distance without stopping. But Rudd's Ford couldn't make it, and with nine laps remaining, the Virginia native dove onto the pit road, turning the lead over to Gordon. Wallace desperately tried to chase him down but fell short. The 1989 Winston Cup champion couldn't believe it. Others, including those in the media, were shaking their heads. They had just seen a monumental roll of the dice that should have produced snake eyes, but instead it had vaulted a team not yet two years old into the spotlight. Jeff Gordon was no longer the inexperienced driver Ray had met in the Busch Series garage. And Ray was no longer the inexperienced crew chief who felt he wasn't good enough. They had both matured in their professions, but it was the inaugural Brickyard 400 at Indianapolis Motor Speedway that would catapult them into international prominence and make them a formidable opponent over the next four years.

FAST FROM THE START

The partnership between Ray Evernham and Jeff Gordon started fast at the 1993 Daytona 500 when Jeff won one of the 125-mile qualifying races.

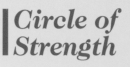

Circle of Strength

TEAM MEETINGS WERE nothing new for those crew members who had spent time with other race teams. If there was time between building cars and testing, the team would meet weekly to evaluate what was wrong and why they lacked consistency. One Tuesday the crew headed for the meeting area expecting another routine critique, but they were met with a surprise. The chairs were arranged in a circle, so instead of most of the group looking at the backs of their teammates' heads, they would face one another. To Ray, this arrangement represented a circle of strength, a spiritual circle resembling the spirit wheel, an item he had found in his many readings on Native Americans.

The circle helped enliven the meetings, and each week the arrangement of the chairs changed to resemble the shape of the track where the next race would be held. In the meetings, Ray would talk with the twenty-five crewmen about what had transpired during the previous race and the team's goals for the upcoming one.

The team continued to bond, and Ray could see it becoming a closer, stronger group. The right people were in place, and now it was essential to motivate them. As their success grew, the meetings became more emotional, and team members began looking forward to them. Eventually, each meeting would reach a point where crewmen would jump out of their seats, shout, and high-five one another.

UNITY

The Rainbow Warriors pit crew evolved into a proud and efficient clan, which, by 1999, had become the standard other crews tried to match.

Going into the first Brickyard 400, Ray felt his team had an advantage because NASCAR had never raced there before. No one had a setup book or years of experience to reference. He contacted several Indy car competitors, including A. J. Foyt and Poncho Carter, asking about the characteristics the track acquired as a race progressed. He searched relentlessly for people who could provide him with tips on what it took to win the Indianapolis 500. When the team tested at the track, it concentrated on the fact that it was fast, flat, and extremely smooth.

In qualifying, Rick Mast had pulled an upset and captured the pole. Gordon had to settle for third behind Earnhardt. But it was the procedures the Rainbow Warriors followed the day before the race that caused the biggest buzz in the garage. Ray had learned through conversations with those who knew the track that it would change as the day progressed. There was no need to participate in Happy Hour, which occurred in the late afternoon. Instead, the team used the noon-to-one practice session to set up its car for the race. It was a decision many people felt was stupid.

There was a special electricity in the Indiana air that race day, the kind that accompanies those moments that people can later recall with complete clarity. Indianapolis authorities had never seen a race crowd so well behaved or so knowledgeable about the sport. The thunder that echoed between the front-stretch grandstands left every true race fan with cold chills on that hot day.

Once the race began, Gordon's competitors quickly realized they had been snookered. Before more than three hundred thousand screaming fans, Gordon, Wallace, and Ernie Irvan diced for the lead. When the final caution flag

> **Drive, Determination and Desire lead to success, not natural talent.**

OVERPOWERING THE COMPETITION

Bottom: Ray and Jeff discussed the setup needed for Martinsville in 1997 where they won the spring race. Facing page: Three years earlier at the inaugural Brickyard 400, they had the perfect setup. Ray incorporated ground effects into the car and learned the track's characteristics late in a race from former Indy 500 winners to set up their victory.

The Brickyard Car

RUMORS HAVE CIRCULATED through the years as to why Jeff Gordon had little difficulty winning the inaugural Brickyard 400, but no one ever came forth with a definitive answer. There was no doubt Gordon, who grew up in nearby Pittsboro, Indiana, wanted to excel in stock car racing's debut at the Indianapolis Motor Speedway. But those searching for his secret have overlooked Ray Evernham's meticulous attention to detail. For Ray, race preparation meant researching the track and translating Indy car technology into stock car setup. Certainly the Chevrolet that the Hendrick Motorsports team raced at the Brickyard in 1994 was a little ahead of its time. Since the track was flat and very smooth, Ray decided the car's setup should incorporate a rear sway bar which helped stabilize the rear end in the flat corners.

Then there were the brake ducts. Ray ordered them mounted differently than they had been before, and in return they provided the bulky car with some ground effects. The brake ducts were located in large corner pans under the front of the car, and they sucked air from beneath its nose. This differed greatly from the common practice of cutting holes in the nose beneath the headlight area to provide cooling air to the brakes. Ray's reasoning was that without holes in the nose, the car's speed and down-force would be much better. Also, the car was raked way over inside the body, so the left-side frame rail was very low compared to the right, which also helped it maneuver at high speed through the flat turns.

waved on lap 132, the lead-lap cars hit the pit road. Wallace's crew performed flawlessly, returning him to the track in the lead. Gordon was second, followed by Irvan. When Wallace slid high and had to slow to keep from hitting the wall, the race had boiled down to Gordon and Irvan. With four laps remaining, Gordon moved to the inside and took the lead as the Robert Yates Racing driver slowed for a right-front flat tire. Jeff Gordon streaked to victory and into the speedway's record books.

During his childhood, Ray had dreamed of driving to victory in the Indianapolis 500. Instead, he ended up directing a young team to victory in the first stock car race ever held on the hallowed track. And when the 1994 season was done, his young but maturing team had an eighth-place finish in the point standings. In just two short years, Ray had turned the team from a nobody into a contender.

In 1994, Ray Evernham and Jeff Gordon achieved every goal they had established for their team. When the 1995 season began, they were right on course with the five-year plan Ray had charted for reaching a Winston Cup championship. All Ray wanted was to improve on their record. That meant increasing the number of victories from two to three and capturing a pole. His private wish list, however, carried more than one pole and five wins as well. Ray knew his team needed the kind of consistency that would allow them to finish in the top five in the Winston Cup point standings. The new Chevrolet Monte Carlo that replaced the Lumina they had raced the previous year proved to be better than anyone expected. Even so, the possibility of winning a championship was not in their thoughts.

It was clear they had the best car at Daytona, but the crew dropped the car off the jack during a pit stop. Gordon, now a mature driver, kept his cool. He simply said over his radio, "Don't worry, guys. I know it's a big race. We're going to have more and we'll get it back." That was the day the team really bonded. The following week at Rockingham, they unveiled the

LOCAL HERO

Victory lane at the first Brickyard 400 in Indianapolis was a dream come true for both Jeff Gordon, top, and Ray, who had once dreamed of driving an Indy Car to victory here.

We built our team
on trust and
honesty and a
burning desire to
be champions.
—RAY EVERNHAM

ROOTS OF SUCCESS

Previous spread: By March 1999 at the inaugural Cracker Barrel 500 in Atlanta, the Rainbow Warriors' pit stops had evolved into a fluid work of art. But it began years before with the pledge they all signed, below, in 1995. When the "Refuse to Lose" T-shirts made their appearance on the pit crew that year, Gordon joined in, top, by hand-lettering his fire-retardant undershirt.

We know How Rough The Road Will Be, How Heavy Here The Load Will Be, We Know About The Barricades That Wait Along The Track, But We Have Set Our Soul Ahead Upon A Certain Goal Ahead And Nothing Left From Hell To Sky Shall Ever Turn Us Back. 5/31/95

"Refuse to Lose" T-shirts Ray had printed and rebounded with a win. The radically different results on back-to-back weekends gave them confidence that they could overcome any obstacle.

At Richmond they got booted out of the penthouse with a fuel pump problem, but they came back with a victory in Atlanta. It was turning into an on-again, off-again season. It seemed as though the team either won or had problems. Though the Hendrick team won half of the first six races, the thought of claiming a championship in only their third season still didn't seem realistic. But by the time the team reached Daytona in July for the Pepsi 400—the race that marks the season's midpoint—they were a victory contender at every event. And when Gordon held off Earnhardt and Sterling Marlin for the Pepsi 400 win, even doubters began changing their attitude. With fifteen of the season's thirty-one races behind

them, the Rainbow Warriors had collected wins on every size oval that composed the Winston Cup circuit—short, intermediate, and superspeedway.

The key to the team's successful preparation was exacting attention to every detail. It wasn't enough to have a finely tuned engine; they had to have a car and a strategy that was tuned to each track. When preparing for a race, Ray analyzed what was important at that track and focused the team's efforts on that area. This way, the team could take full advantage of everything it could do to ready itself for that specific event. Tuning a car at the track and getting it to perform at its peak were Ray's areas of expertise.

Analyzing the difference between the one-mile track at Loudon, New Hampshire, and the 1.366-mile track at Darlington, South Carolina, Ray decided track position was the most important thing at Loudon, while at Darlington it was all about tire wear. Track position at Loudon is critical because the cars run so close to one another and it's extremely difficult to pass. Ray also paid special attention to the brakes and to how well a car turned in the middle of the corner.

At Darlington, the key was to have a car that could run five hundred miles and not blow the engine or pack the radiator full of sand and rubber and overheat. On the road courses, the transmission is the key. The proper gearing will allow the car to always stay in its power range. At Charlotte, it was essential to have a car that was not loose getting into turn three and that would turn well as it exited turn four. If those two issues were solved, getting through turns one and two quickly would be no problem.

In the season's second half, the Rainbow Warriors won three more times as Ray's team finally found the consistency it had sought. Earnhardt couldn't shake them with the mind games he played so well, as Ray thwarted him at every turn. Ray became more intense, more focused simply on what needed to be done on a race-to-race basis. His team concentrated on the task facing them, with quick, consistent work on pit road playing a key role in each race. The decision to hire a pit crew coach three years earlier was paying major dividends every weekend. In the season's final race at Atlanta, both drivers did what they needed to do. Earnhardt won the race and led most of the way. Gordon, despite an ill-handling car, led for one lap and defeated Earnhardt by 34 points for the Rainbow Warriors' first Winston Cup championship.

Ray was speechless, nearly in shock, that sunny November day as he claimed his first-ever championship as a crew chief. When Ray had agreed to become Jeff's crew chief, he had established a five-year plan for winning the championship. He had never dreamed it could be accomplished in three. In his heart, Ray felt the team had claimed a championship it probably wasn't ready to win. In racing, there is an adage that before a team can win a championship it must lose one. Evernham and his team, however, did the reverse.

I think the 24 team is the team to beat.
Jeff Gordon is a great driver, but you
have to remember, he has a great team.
—DALE EARNHARDT, SEVEN-TIME NASCAR
WINSTON CUP CHAMPION

DO *one thing every day that makes you a little better at your job.*

They won one before they lost one. And the one they lost in 1996, to teammate Terry Labonte, despite a ten-win season, taught them what they needed to do to return to the top. Ray learned through that experience that constant innovation was what would keep them ahead of the competition. He decided he needed to know more about racing, and so after the season ended, he went to Frank Hawley's well-known drag racing school in Gainesville, Florida.

Ray was one of only two students who passed the class and was awarded his Top Alcohol license. He had never driven a dragster before, but he ran the quarter mile in 6.56 seconds at 208 miles per hour. He had gone to the school to try to get a broader picture of racing; what he learned was the importance of thinking smaller. Ray learned how differently drag racers looked at time. On the NASCAR circuit, drivers and crew were thinking in terms of tenths of seconds over the course of a race that lasts for two to three hours. A drag race is often over in less than five seconds, and drivers and crews agonize over trying to cut a thousandth of a second from their times. He went back to the garage and began to look at everything in a smaller way. How could they gain half a horsepower, half a count of drag? He looked once again at the aerodynamics, the chassis, and the tire pressure. On the superspeedways, restrictor plate racing is so close, the cars so evenly matched, that Ray reasoned the gain of a thousandth of a second here and there was well worth the effort. He was proved right when the Rainbow Warriors went to Daytona to open the 1997 season and won the Daytona 500.

RAY J TODDLED along his parents' blue stone driveway, occasionally placing his hands on it in an effort to keep his balance. He'd just started learning to walk in June 1992, about a month shy of his first birthday. That night while preparing her son for bed, Mary Evernham noticed little bruises on the palms of his hands.

He had been running a low-grade fever since the Fourth of July and refused to put weight on his left leg when he walked. The doctors couldn't decide what was wrong, but nothing seemed alarming until one morning when Mary walked into Ray J's room and found tiny broken blood vessels all over his legs, arms, cheeks, even inside his ears. The doctor found that all of his organs, including his liver, were enlarged. Blood work and a spinal tap revealed Acute Lymphocytic Leukemia.

The diagnosis sent their lives into a tailspin. They had planned to be reunited in North Carolina that summer. Mary had quit her job days earlier. The family immediately headed for New York, where Ray J began chemotherapy. His treatment lasted two and a half years, although he was in remission slightly more than a month after the diagnosis.

Mary and Ray J moved to North Carolina in January 1993, and he continued treatment in Chapel Hill. They flew to New York each month so Ray J could undergo a bone aspiration to confirm if any cancer remained in his system. Ray plunged into his work even deeper. The stress of career and family changes was overwhelming. Ray J's illness put a heavy strain on their marriage, but Mary, who had stood by him through so many things, once again helped him through it.

Ray J's disease remained in remission, but Ray's heart had been touched by the struggles of his son and the other children he'd met during that time. During 600 Week at Charlotte in 1994, Ray helped the Red Cross and the Leukemia Society promote a donor drive, registering race members of the motorsports community for the Bone Marrow Society donor-match database. Afterward, he wrote a personal thank-you note to each of the more than ninety people who registered.

In the last race of the 1995 season at Atlanta, the Rainbow Warriors ran a second car with a Leukemia Society paint scheme in honor of a young girl who had passed away from the disease. Their theme for that race was "Racing for a Reason," with the car's winnings donated to the Leukemia Society. Ray still supports charities and research connected with leukemia, as does Rick Hendrick, who, in 1998, became a leukemia survivor himself.

It took two or three years for Ray to come to the point where he could talk to other parents about this experience. He has since counseled parents who are facing the nightmare he and Mary and Ray J did.

"I don't know," Ray has said, "if that was a lesson from God to help me deal with the rest of my life, or maybe to help other people, but the worst fear I've had in my life is having to deal with the possible loss of a child."

Racing for a Reason

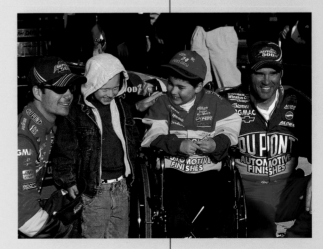

BATTLERS

Ray and Jeff provided some special time for these children in 1999. Following spread: The start of the 1996 Brickyard 400 featured pole-sitter Jeff Gordon (24) and Mark Martin (6) in the first row, but 24th-qualifier Dale Jarrett won the race.

How we met wasn't by luck. It was truly by God's blessing and fate.
—JEFF GORDON

We go to the
track to win, not
just to race.
—RAY EVERNHAM

VERSATILITY

From short tracks such as

Martinsville, Virginia, top,

to winding road courses like

Sears Point, California,

bottom, the Rainbow

Warriors eventually

conquered them all.

Ten thousand people hold a NASCAR license. There were twenty-five Rainbow Warriors.

—RAY EVERNHAM

The Rainbow Warriors were determined to anticipate every problem and to deal with each obstacle as well as the pressure that accompanied a title bout. They became the first team to have its driver win on every type of track on the Winston Cup circuit in a single season. They had now won just about everything NASCAR had on the schedule: the Busch Clash, the Daytona 500, the Winston, the Winston Million, the Coca-Cola 600, the inaugural race at California Speedway, and a record three straight Southern 500s. With ten wins in 1997, they became the first team to produce back-to-back double-digit victory seasons since car owner Junior Johnson and his driver Darrell Waltrip in 1981–1982.

No one could point to a single reason for the Rainbow Warriors' success. Sometimes a race might be won with a clever pit call, while another time it might be through good communication, or the fastest car. That's what makes Winston Cup racing unique. There are so many different tracks and scenarios that the same setup, strategy, or racing tactic won't win every week.

By now there was no secret to the success the Rainbow Warriors enjoyed: it was through attention to detail. They had a plan; they worked on the details; and they had the best of everything in personnel and equipment. Still, earning a second straight championship wasn't easy. Not all the pressure came from inside the garage, as Gordon, now in his midtwenties, had become the driver many fans loved to hate. The team's success brought jeers, and any misfortune inspired lusty cheers. Some even accused NASCAR of playing favorites with the team. Yet the sanctioning body often changed rules during the season in ways that weren't in Ray's favor. And NASCAR told Ray not to return with the innovative car he used to win the Winston for the second time in three years. This was a car the Rainbow Warriors called "T-Rex," and it was, as Ray would say with a slight smile, "ahead of its time." Ray had worked with engineer Rex Stump to develop a car that was set up to take maximum advantage of its rigidity, handling, and aerodynamics, as well as the placement of some of its components. It was not an illegal car, but Ray had taken advantage of things that weren't written in the rules—yet. When NASCAR rewrote the rules, the 3-by-5-inch chassis tubing T-Rex had was outside the new specs, as were the way the snout was connected to the front frame rail and the height of the floor pan and roll bars, among other things.

In the season's closing months, the pressure the team faced from Dale Jarrett and Mark Martin in the championship battle became almost unbearable. Entering the season's final race, the Rainbow Warriors had a seventy-seven-point lead over Jarrett and were eighty-seven points ahead of Martin. Naturally, they took one of their best cars to Atlanta, but in the first practice Gordon spun on the pit road while trying to put heat in his tires and hit Bobby Hamilton's Pontiac, which was stopped. Both teams had to pull their backup cars off the transporters. In a race-morning meeting, Ray's team agreed not to take any unnecessary chances. All it had to do to secure its second championship was finish eighteenth or better. Gordon came home seventeenth to win the closest three-way battle in Winston Cup history.

The next season, 1998, began with high expectations, but nearly fizzled in the first half. One could say that the Rainbow Warriors were on cruise control once the season reached mid-June. Up until that point, they had collected only three wins and three poles. In the Winston, Ray accidentally ran the car out of fuel as it headed for turn one on the final lap. A few fans unleashed their disappointment on Ray as he and Mary left the track, yelling obscenities and throwing beer at them. But three weeks later, after finishing thirty-seventh at Richmond because of an accident, the team went on a top-five rampage that left the Winston Cup circuit in shambles. In the last twenty races they finished outside the top five only once, and even the Phoenix race would probably have been a top-five finish had the event not been shortened by rain.

But the team's unbelievable performance wasn't based on mere luck. It grew out of three events during the season that fired up the Rainbow Warriors and made them unstoppable. At Charlotte in May, Jeff missed a Saturday-morning practice and

CONQUERING THE BRICKYARD

Below: Ray and Jeff celebrated their second Brickyard 400 win in five years in 1998. They won the inaugural race in 1994.

SPECIAL MOMENTS

Previous spread: Jeff

Gordon and the Rainbow

Warriors celebrated their

vicotory in the 1988

Southern 500 which netted

Jeff the Winston Million

bonus. Below: Ray cele-

brated NASCAR's 50th

anniversary with his dad,

Ray Sr., after clinching the

1998 championship. Top:

Ray, Jeff, and Jeff's wife,

Brooke, prayed on pit road

with chaplain Max Helton

prior to their 1999

125-mile qualifying

race at Daytona.

Terry Labonte briefly drove the number 24 in that session, tagging the wall with it. That got Gordon's focus channeled in the right direction. After he was spun out by Rusty Wallace at Richmond in June and finished thirty-seventh, he told Ray he was determined not to let Wallace—or any driver, for that matter—keep him from the championship. The team felt they had something to prove and reached down each week for that little bit extra.

No longer did people ask if the Rainbow Warriors could win a race. Now the question was whether anyone could come close to beating them. From mid-July until mid-August, the Rainbow Warriors won every race on the schedule. The win streak included a second victory in the Brickyard 400 and pushed their season total to eight. No matter what the other teams did, they couldn't find a way to defeat the Rainbow Warriors. If others changed four tires, Ray ordered only two. If they tried to beat Ray with his own strategy with a two-tire change late in the race, he would turn the tables and give Gordon four fresh ones.

The competitors' frustration exploded in August after Ray guided his team to their tenth win at New Hampshire. Jack Roush accused the Rainbow Warriors of illegally soaking tires to make them softer for the short, late-race runs. By the time the circuit reached Darlington on Labor Day weekend for the Southern 500, "Tiregate" consumed the headlines. The accusation infuriated Ray, who was now determined to run his opposition into the ground. Each day at the track, if the outline of his jawbone was visible, it was best just to turn and walk the other way. Socializing had never been allowed on the number 24 truck. It was a workplace, and now no one dared step onto the back of the hauler without an invitation or a public relations escort. The team picked up on the cue and redoubled their determination. At Darlington in September, it was so hot that Gordon threw up during a pit stop, but his determination to win carried the team to the checkered flag and a Winston Million dollar bonus.

By the time the season ended, the Rainbow Warriors had won three of the last four races to bring their victory total to thirteen, tying Richard Petty's record for the modern era. Yet while Gordon emerged from his third championship season in four years in better emotional condition than in the previous year, Ray didn't. His intensity had skyrocketed in 1998, and he spent every minute working to gain an advantage. He considered himself the leader of the best team in motorsports, the team that fielded a car for the best driver, and it was his responsibility to make sure his driver had the best of everything. He had begun feeling that it was time to take the next step in his career. The success of the Rainbow Warriors had made them unpopular with many racing fans whose own heroes seemingly could no longer compete. They had become like the Yankees, the team many fans loved to hate. It's not easy to work constantly in the public eye, and Ray had reached the point where it was difficult to shrug off the jeers that erupted from the grandstands when his team had a problem or was involved in an accident.

There was pressure to get better every week, even when the team was winning a third of the races on the circuit. Ray wondered if he was being realistic. In his heart, he knew that even Jeff Gordon didn't need him the way he once did, and he was weary of being a crew chief. He was losing his focus, and that was a terrible feeling for Ray. He no longer felt creative or clever. It was difficult to muster enthusiasm for the 1999 season when the time arrived. He was still exhausted from the previous campaign and needed something to rejuvenate him. Earlier in his career, defeat and injury had furnished the turning points in Ray's life. He had worked his way through the setbacks this time, just as he always had. He had overcome the personal and professional obstacles to rise to the top of his profession, and it was his success that now was nagging at him. Change was in the wind.

CREATE *something special for your people to be a part of.*

BRICKYARD MEMENTO

This license plate commemorates Ray's first two victories in 1994. Note the Hendrick Acura designation. That's because Ray actually talked team owner Rick Hendrick out of the car—an Acura NSX—after the team won the Coca Cola 600 and the inaugural Brickyard 400.

FIRST CHAMPIONSHIP

In 1995, Ray reaped his first Winston Cup championship, commemorated by this plate attached to a Dodge Viper.

TITLE II

After bowing to Hendrick Motorsports teammate Terry Labonte in 1996, Ray rebounded with his team to capture their second Winston Cup title in three years, and Ray's Plymouth Prowler now carries this plate.

THIRD TIME'S A CHARM

The Rainbow Warriors' dominating season championship in 1998 is commemorated by this plate on Ray's Harley-Davidson motorcycle.

Garage Full of Memories

I could finally say that I did it. I did something big in racing. But I won't say that, because I know that I didn't do it. What I will say is that we did it.

—Ray Evernham

LIFE *is not easy.* *It's not supposed to be.*

TEAMWORK

Previous spread: Ray plotted

strategy with Jeff Gordon at

Sears Point in June 1999

Below (left to right): Team

owner Rick Hendrick, Jeff

Gordon, Rick's father "Papa

Joe" Hendrick, and Ray

celebrated a victory in

Atlanta. The bond these

men developed during the

Rainbow Warriors era is

one Ray has cherished

over the years.

FINISHING WINNERS

Facing page: Ray and Jeff

won the last race Ray

crew- chiefed for Gordon, a

Busch Series race at

Phoenix in 1999.

Ray and Jeff Gordon had announced in October 1998 that they would field a Busch team for a limited schedule the following year. Publicly, it was to keep Pepsi involved with Jeff and give the corporation its own car on the track, something it hadn't had since the early 1980s on the Winston Cup circuit. Really, the two men wanted to see how they worked together when they shared ownership. Dodge officials had approached them in late 1998 about leaving Hendrick Motorsports and joining their camp. Ray and Jeff wouldn't discuss it with Dodge while they went for their third title. The Busch deal let them test the waters without showing their hand.

The Rainbow Warriors opened the 1999 season with a win in the Daytona 500. On the heels of that came a win at Atlanta, and slightly more than a month later, another at California. But this time Dale Jarrett, Bobby Labonte, Jeff Burton, Dale Earnhardt, and a rookie named Tony Stewart were forcing Gordon to share the victory spotlight. Ray and Jeff decided not to pursue the Dodge deal together. But Dodge officials returned to Ray and asked him to consider doing it on his own. He agonized over whether to leave Gordon and Hendrick, but finally concluded the Monday after the race at Richmond in September that it was something he had to do.

For six years, Ray was engulfed in making the team successful, and it had consumed his thoughts. He didn't want to win just one race; he wanted all of them. And the Rainbow Warriors had succeeded beyond all expectations. Sadly, Ray has scant recollection of what actually happened. He never stopped to smell the roses of success before moving to the next objective.

Ray called Jeff at home to give him the news. Then he drove to Rick's South Charlotte home for an emotional meeting spiced with memories of their run of success that had seemed to pass all too quickly. Ray was trading the now-famous multicolored uniform of the Rainbow Warriors for Dodge red, ending one of the most successful driver–crew chief relationships in NASCAR history. As Rick Hendrick's door closed behind him that night, a new door was opening in front of Ray. But as he walked toward his car, what was on his mind wasn't the impossibly short time he had to prepare a new team for his next challenge. He was thinking back across an impossibly short trip from a rutted, imaginary race track in his childhood backyard in New Jersey to the victory lane on the world's fastest superspeedways.

Once he had reached the pinnacle of championships and the success he found as a crew chief, it was time for him to move on and do something different.

—RICK HENDRICK

Reduced Weight

BUILDING IT RIGHT

The cramped world of the driver enclosed Jeff Gordon, right, in a car designed with only speed and safety in mind. Following spread: Ray took rookie driver Casey Atwood (19) to three races in 2000 in a car sponsored by Motorola. At Martinsville in October, Atwood found himself dueling with Tony Stewart (20).

WEIGHT REDUCTION IS best done when a car is built, not afterward. Ray's goal with weight is to build the car so that it has the right weight percentages and can still carry some ballast. The car must weigh 3,400 pounds— 3,600 pounds with a driver. The quest is not simply about making the car light; it's about making it light in the right places. To do this, Ray's team must consider unsprung weight, which makes it handle better, and rotating weight, which makes a car accelerate faster. And the basic answer to the weight problem is efficiency. A bolt doesn't have to be any longer than is required for the job. Even the number of pop rivets is considered.

Safety and cost are also important factors in weight reduction. The cost rises whenever a team selects an exotic metal or composite

material or runs up added time on the problem. And then there are the fines. NASCAR levied its largest fine ever on May 30, 1995, when it assessed a sixty-thousand-dollar fine against Ray and placed him on indefinite probation for using an unapproved right-front hub in the Coca-Cola 600 at Charlotte. The hub wasn't intended to circumvent safety standards; in fact, it wasn't even supposed to be on the car during the race. It had been installed for qualifying.

Driver safety is vital. The team can't risk having something fall off during a race. Ray doesn't believe in drilling more holes than are already designed into the equipment just to reduce weight. Practicing engineering basics produces parts that are lighter, stronger, and safer without adding the weakening effects of holes.

I was drawn to Ray before I ever knew him. You can tell just from watching him that he has talent for what he does. I was nervous about moving up to Winston Cup, but I know I have the best behind me.
—Casey Atwood, NASCAR's Young Gun

NEW VISION

BARELY A DAY after his release from Hendrick Motorsports, Ray Evernham sat in the office area at Gordon-Evernham Motorsports

in Concord, North Carolina, while hammers pounded and saws whined overhead. Workers scurried to build offices for Ray because

the three Dodge teams—Ray's new factory team, Evernham Motorsports, along with Petty Enterprises and Bill Davis Racing—had

less than two years to develop Dodge's Winston Cup entry. That included getting a car and an engine approved by NASCAR,

building and testing the cars, and in some cases, hiring the drivers. If Ray's cell phone wasn't ringing, his answering machine was

recording. In less than an hour, three Winston Cup drivers wanting to be considered for the new opportunity had left messages.

Meanwhile, just a few days after Ray left, the Rainbow Warriors once again celebrated in victory lane at Martinsville. Ray

was happy for Brian Whitesell, the new crew chief, and for Jeff Gordon. He was proud of Jeff and the team, because it seemed

as though so many people were waiting for them to fail. To Ray, the proof of having been a good manager was that he had built

something that remained successful after he left. Gordon's win eased some of the pain he felt at leaving and gave him a little

more confidence that he could start over and do it all again with Dodge.

I've never really cared about much but racing. Mary has been that anchor to things you're supposed to do with family and friends, you know, real life.

—RAY EVERNHAM

FAMILY

Top: Nobody tears up the Evernham backyard with cars and motorcycles, but life is still fun when Mary, Ray, and Ray J are together. Bottom: Ray winds down after work with a ride on his Harley. Facing page: Unlike his Dad, Ray J is far more interested in playing the piano than racing cars.

Dodge's official announcement regarding its return to Winston Cup racing and the role Ray would play was still two weeks away, but he wasted no time in turning his dream into reality. He had found what he needed to reenergize himself. It would also allow him to have some family time. When Ray began with the number 24 team for Rick Hendrick, Ray J was twelve months old and battling leukemia. Now he was eight, the disease was in remission, and he could sit beside his father and read a book. Ray J had gone from infant to boy without his father by his side. Ray had been racing all those years, and now it was time to slow down and catch up to his own family.

> **IF** *you give someone a project, give him or her guidance, resources, and time frames, and let them go.*

Ray knew that in order to build his new team he needed a well-known veteran driver who had enjoyed success on the Winston Cup circuit. Since Jeff Gordon wasn't available, Ray's first choice was Bill Elliott. He had a lot of faith in the 1988 Winston Cup champion, and he felt Elliott could help him build the organization if he could be patient during the process.

By the time the Winston Cup circuit reached Phoenix in 1999, rumors already had Bill Elliott divesting himself of his team at the end of the 2000 season and joining Ray's operation. Finally, at Atlanta Motor Speedway on March 10, 2000, Ray stepped to the podium in the track's infield media center and confirmed what had been the worst-kept secret on the circuit. For the first time in his racing career, Elliott would drive something other than a Ford. Bill was the perfect person to partner with Ray because he already had a facility and held provisional starting positions that could be used in the first four races of 2001. He also had the experience of having built an operation and could be an adviser in some of the business aspects as well.

LIKE FATHER, LIKE SON Ray has always been mischievous, and Ray J is no different. At Rockingham in 1998, one of many races Ray J has attended, he decided his dad didn't need to see what was going on.

Ray couldn't stop smiling as he announced he had signed Elliott to a multiyear contract beginning in 2001. Winston Cup team owner Mark Melling then joined Elliott and Ray on stage to reveal that he had agreed to release the number 9 to Evernham Motorsports. That would allow Elliott to complete his career with the car number he had used when he enjoyed so much success with Melling's late father,

Harry, winning the Winston Million in 1985 and the 1988 Winston Cup championship. It was a banner day for Ray, who had now achieved half of his goal: a veteran driver for his operation. Not even the chilly March weather could dispel the warmth that Ray, Bill, and Dodge officials felt about their coup.

When Ray told him he wanted to team him with a very young, rookie driver, Awesome Bill recommended Casey Atwood. Atwood had done some testing for Elliott, and the veteran was impressed with him. Once Ray talked with Atwood, he realized the young man had a good understanding of what he felt in a race car and what he needed to feel. Now the task was to get Atwood a car to race.

After he returned from Atlanta in March, Ray was shocked when a NASCAR official appeared at his shop with a set of templates. Dodge officials had wanted their entry to maintain the character lines of its passenger car, but what Ray found himself looking at now was a set of existing NASCAR templates. Ray had already built two Dodge Intrepids and tested one in the wind tunnel.

Ray's team had little choice this late in the game. They built the new car using the NASCAR templates as a guideline, but working with Dodge officials, they made some changes. NASCAR returned and made a new set of templates off that car. That is why the Ford and Dodge templates are so close to each other even though they were made from two different cars. NASCAR's decision rendered the two Intrepids that Ray and Petty Enterprises had built useless. One was cut up and the other eventually became a test car.

While working to develop a car that met NASCAR's criteria, Ray turned the 13,000-square-foot building that once housed Gordon-Evernham Motorsports into a Winston Cup engine shop and the marketing headquarters for Evernham Motorsports. He leased another building in the industrial park beside the Mooresville, North Carolina, dragstrip and developed the Dodge's chassis and body there. Only a few people knew the access code to the room where a bank of computers sat, linked directly to Dodge headquarters in Michigan.

On the other side of the building sat a Chevrolet Monte Carlo that Ray had built so he could conduct a comparison test with the Dodge. Elliott provided a Ford, while Petty had a Pontiac, so Ray could see how the new program stacked up against all three cars. Ray also made frequent trips to Elliott's shop in Statesville., which would become the primary shop for Evernham Motorsports in December 2000. The new Dodge's first on-track shakedown was May 2, 2000, at

TEAMWORK

The new Dodge team's most visible member was probably veteran driver and former team owner Bill Elliott, top, but it also included Dodge engineers behind the scenes who were developing a brand-new engine for the race track, bottom.

The Imaginary Wind Tunnel

When refining a car in the wind tunnel, the key is to know a track's characteristics and demands. For example, the most important element at Daytona is drag. For Ray Evernham, eliminating drag means more than simply studying the numbers from the wind tunnel. It means imagining the airflow over and under the high-powered machine.

After testing a car, Ray will stand for hours in front of it and take photographs and silhouettes in an effort to find any little bump, any minute piece of sheet metal, that might adversely affect the wind flow. Then he crawls under the car and, like a crime scene investigator, spends hours searching for marks on the chassis or evidence of sandblasting.

The ability to visualize the wind and a car's reaction to it, as well as to the race track itself, is a gift. It allows Ray to understand a car's suspension, or how the wind whips around its sleek body. Many times he has closed his eyes and, in his mind, turned the car into a cartoon speeding around a corner.

When Jeff Gordon would explain to Ray how the car felt to him, the former driver would close his eyes and make believe he could see the car's suspension and its tires moving.

Even with his current drivers and crew chiefs, Ray still creates a mental picture of how the car is reacting to the track—how the shock absorbers are working, the wheels are turning, and the driveshaft is performing. He describes it as having "built-in ESPN," a gift that makes it much easier to correct a problem with a car.

Virtual Racing

A one-third-scale clay model of the Dodge body provided the first wind tunnel test of the car's aerodynamics, top. A computer animation known as a CATIA drawing also helped Ray and the Dodge engineers see how their new Intrepid R/T might behave during an actual race.

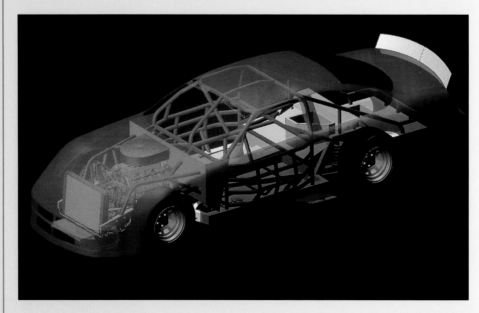

BUILT FROM SCRATCH
While Ray and the
Dodge team worked at
the design of the new
Dodge body, left and
below right, Engineers,
below left, designed
not just a new intake
manifold but an entirely
new Dodge engine for
racing in only five
hundred days.

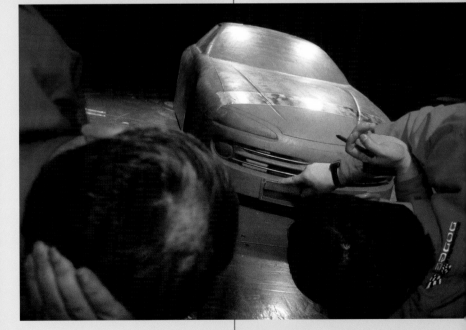

Homestead, Florida. There, Dodge's engineering staff was introduced and the company's one-team concept approach explained in detail. The car had yet to be approved by NASCAR, but it was not quite ready for submission.

A few days before the Coca-Cola 600, Ray called the media to victory lane at Lowe's Motor Speedway to formally announce his second driver. Since they knew no one would be surprised, his team decided to turn the announcement into a skit. Standing in victory lane, Ray called Casey on his cell phone and asked if he was on his way to the track. The premise was supposed to be that Casey couldn't find his way to victory lane and needed a veteran to show him. By the time Atwood, with Elliott in the passenger seat, drove through the banner at the back of victory lane in a charcoal-colored Viper, the wind had blown the script out of Ray's hands and scattered it among the media. The large banner fell and hit Elliott in the head as they passed through it, leaving the actors and audience to dissolve in laughter.

Ray had managed to hire both of the drivers he wanted, but the business side of running a race team and dealing with driver contracts sent him back to the books. This time, instead of reaching for coaching and philosophy books, he was studying business and accounting. But he couldn't concentrate strictly on his own team while he still had a program to spearhead through NASCAR's approval process. The engine designed for the program went to the dynamometer for the first time in late May 2000, but it didn't get its first on-track test until mid-July at Kentucky Speedway. While Ray, Petty, and Davis concentrated on the technical aspects of the program, Dodge officials negotiated with two other teams. They announced in June that Melling Racing and Stacy Compton would join Dodge. Chad Knaus, whom Ray had initially hired to be Atwood's crew chief, would be moved to Melling's operation to serve in that position for Compton.

On August 4, just two days before Ray submitted the Dodge Intrepid R/T body to NASCAR, Chip Ganassi announced that the team he had purchased from Felix Sabates would switch from Chevrolet to Dodge, and Ernie Elliott would provide the team with its engines. NASCAR finally

YOUNG GUN

Rookie driver Casey Atwood, facing page was Dodge's new face on the circuit. With Ray's team coming into its own behind him, Atwood figured to develop as a force in future years. Following spread: By May 2000, Kyle Petty drove the first on-track tests in the new Dodge at Homestead Speedway in Florida.

approved the Dodge body on August 29, and the teams were able to start building cars for the 2001 season. Ray could breathe a brief sigh of relief before heading to Richmond with Atwood for his Winston Cup debut.

It wasn't until September 27 that a cylinder block, cylinder heads, three intake manifolds, a water manifold, head gasket, water pump, and fuel pump were given to NASCAR for its examination. Dodge's superspeedway car received its first test in mid-October at Talladega, but since the engine hadn't been approved, only the car's aerodynamics could be tweaked.

NOTHING *great is* *ever accomplished alone.*

TECHNOLOGY

The engine in the new Dodge race car did not exist before 2000 and was designed and built specifically for the Intrepid R/T Winston Cup car in less than a year.

Tension mounted among the Dodge teams as the various drivers took turns participating in the tests. Finally, in November, not even two months before testing was to begin in January at Daytona, NASCAR signed off on Dodge's engine. The new engine's durability was still a big question mark, but now Ray could concentrate on preparing his two racing teams for the 2001 season. In early January, those attending Lowe's Motor Speedway's annual media tour headed for Ray's 43,000-square-foot Statesville shop. He had accepted the keys to the building from Elliott shortly after the 2000 season ended, and with that exchange, the lengthy workdays that had consumed his life at the number 24 shop had returned.

Ray laid out his plan, determining what positions he needed to fill first, before he began hiring employees. He listed his first choice for each position, then went after those people. In instances where he couldn't get whomever he wanted, he knew he would have to train others to become the employees he desired. Ray knew that the correct chemistry wasn't going to happen overnight. He also knew that everyone who helped him start Evernham Motorsports had paid a price, and it had not been a lot of fun.

By the first week of January, nine race cars had been completed and five taken to the wind tunnel. Ray's goal was to have seventeen cars built by the time the teams headed for Speedweeks a month later. For the season, they would need fourteen for each team and two spares—a speedway car and a downforce car.

Becoming a team owner was a humbling experience for Ray. He swept floors at the shop; helped hang bulletin boards, pictures, and shelves on the walls;

TEST TIME

Dodge's first on-track test came at Homestead-Miami Speedway in May 2000. Kyle Petty, top (in car) drove the test Dodge Intrepid. (Left to right) Ray, Dodge executive Lou Patane, and team owner Bill Davis studied the car. The new Dodge and the old, bottom, took to the course during Dodge's first on-track engine test at Talladega Superspeedway the day after the Winston 500 in October 2000.

The Number 9 Car

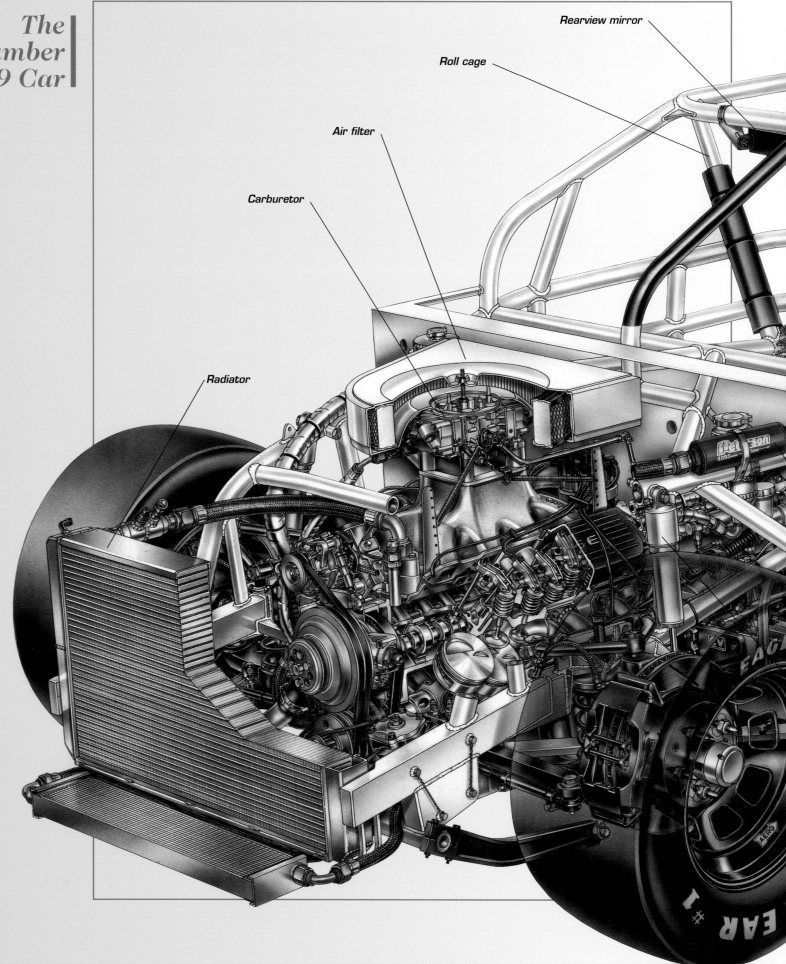

Rearview mirror

Roll cage

Air filter

Carburetor

Radiator

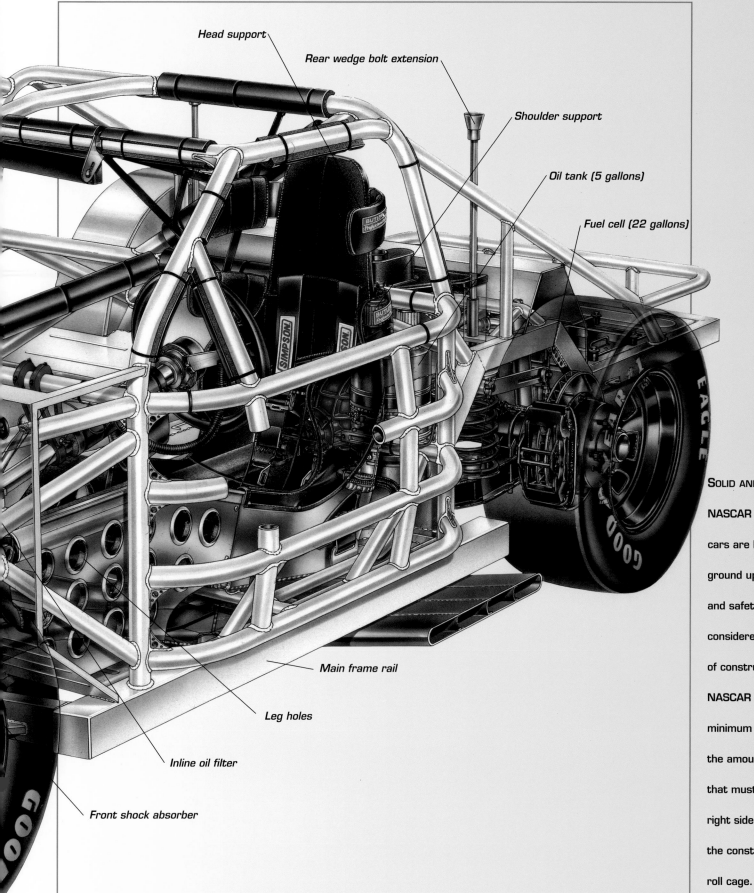

Head support

Rear wedge bolt extension

Shoulder support

Oil tank (5 gallons)

Fuel cell (22 gallons)

Main frame rail

Leg holes

Inline oil filter

Front shock absorber

SOLID AND SAFE

NASCAR Winston Cup
cars are built from the
ground up, with weight
and safety equipment
considered at the time
of construction.
NASCAR dictates the
minimum weight and
the amount of weight
that must go on the
right side, as well as
the construction of the
roll cage.

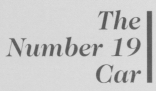

The Number 19 Car

BUILT FOR SPEED

The Dodge Intrepid R/T looks fast even sitting still. Development of the car incorporated good downforce with as little drag as possible. Its sleek design made it immediately compatible with the superspeedways at Daytona and Talladega.

Windshield support bars

350 c.u. in. 700 hp engine

Front air dam

Engine oil cooler

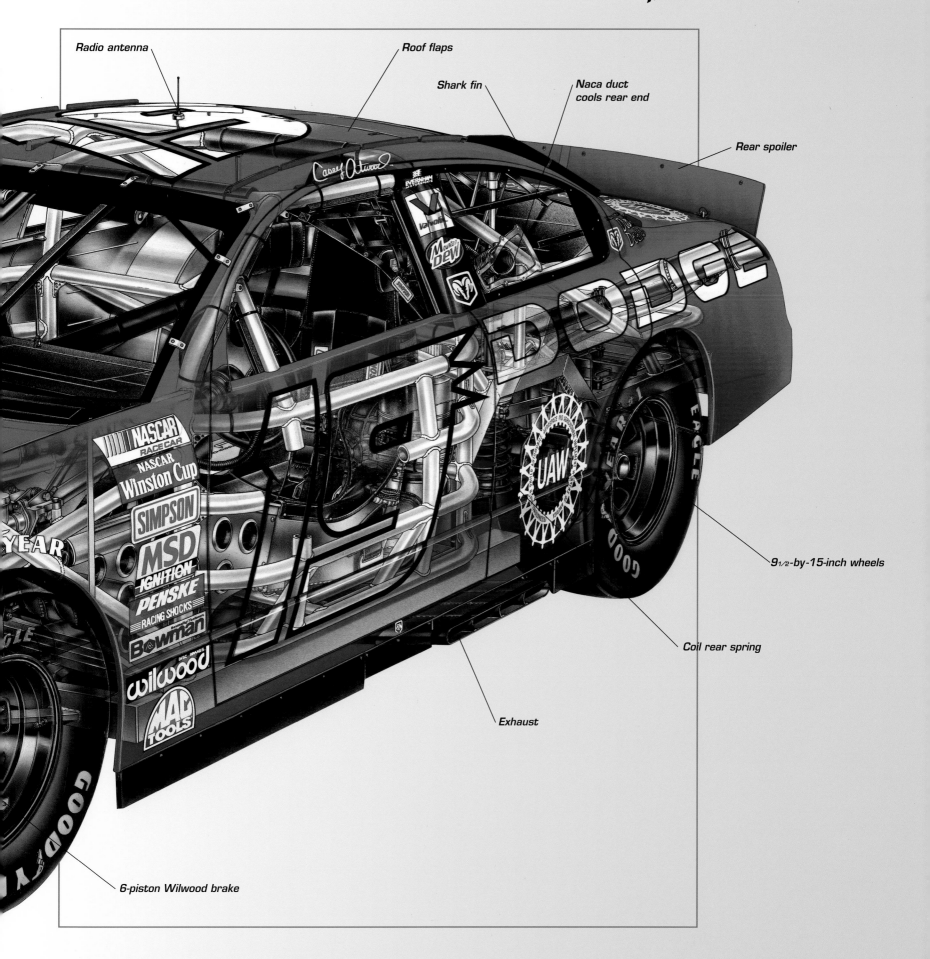

Radio antenna

Roof flaps

Shark fin

Naca duct
cools rear end

Rear spoiler

9½-by-15-inch wheels

Coil rear spring

Exhaust

6-piston Wilwood brake

and worked tirelessly with his crewmen in the shop doing Bondo work on the Daytona car and showing fabricators how he wanted tailpipes constructed and seats and belts mounted. He helped load the transporter before it left for a wind tunnel test. Sometimes members of the team have had to run him out of the way. It is a challenge of an entirely different magnitude than any Ray has encountered before to manage and motivate 120 people and to help direct them onto his philosophical road. It can be exhausting and frustrating, but his vision for his operation has never waned.

ON THE MOVE

In their inaugural season, Dodge and Evernham Motorsports led several races while collecting top-five and top-ten finishes.

Making the transition from crew chief to car owner wasn't easy. Ray was most comfortable with the car building and racing end of the business; the administrative side was a continuing challenge. Very quickly, Ray realized he knew nothing about this part of the job. He dove into accounting and business books. He sought out Rick Hendrick, Richard Childress, Andy Petree, Bill Davis, and Richard Petty for advice. He kept detailed notes and negotiated several sponsor contracts.

Ray knew his reputation and financial future hinged on the outcome of the Dodge program and the performance of his two race teams. Never one to accept an average performance or effort, he was also a realist, and that meant setting realistic goals for the first season. For Elliott, a finish in the top fifteen in points and challenging for wins and poles by the end of the season would be acceptable. For Atwood, the goal was to stay in a tight battle for rookie honors.

By the time the Dodge teams had made their way to Daytona for Speedweeks 2001, they had only

the last few of the five hundred days to prepare for their first day on the job: the Daytona 500. Unlike the other Dodge teams, Evernham Motorsports was a fledgling organization. The drivers and crew had a lot of individual racing experience, but none as a team under the fire of real competition. No one, least of all Ray, knew what to expect. The weeks before qualifying had been nerve-racking for the team, as they encountered difficulties with their cars' aerodynamics on the superspeedway. Ray and Elliott's crew chief, Mike Ford, spent a lot of time in the body shop and the wind tunnel trying to find that last few miles an hour that would make the cars competitive. By the time qualifying day arrived, Ray may not have been completely confident in the final outcome, but he was satisfied they had done all they could to prepare.

HAVE *compassion for your people.*

Every racing fan knows what happened next. Bill Elliott had once won three straight poles at Daytona, but that had been more than a dozen years before. As he circled the track in his first qualifying run in a Dodge, he felt as though the car was jumping around on him and, to the veteran driver, his speed didn't seem fast enough. He shut down his engine after crossing the finish line and the voice of Mike Ford broke the sudden silence in the coasting race car. When Ford announced his speed, 183.565 miles per hour, Elliott couldn't believe it. After twelve years, he had once again won the pole at

To be a champion it takes an uncompromising commitment. . . . I have no doubt Ray will bring the same type of championship commitment he displayed as a crew chief to Evernham Motorsports as an owner.
—BILL PARCELLS, TWO-TIME SUPER BOWL WINNING COACH

Daytona. The effect on Ray was numbing. It was almost an anticlimax for the new car owner, and deep inside he had the same feeling he'd had when the Rainbow Warriors won their first Winston Cup title—it seemed to come too quickly. As they walked back to the media center after qualifying was done, Bill kidded Ray gently: "You're the boss, now. You'd better sit down and get some rest. You're going to need it before the week's over." But all Ray could do was worry that this success might give everything a false perspective, making it seem too easy, and perhaps provide the fans with unrealistic expectations.

The real success this day was broader, though perhaps less spectacular, than winning the pole. All the Dodge teams had qualified, and behind Elliott and Compton, Dodge had the top two spots in the field. After a twenty-year absence, Dodge had reentered NASCAR with engines less than a year old. Regardless of the outcome of this race or the ones that followed, Ray had once again been part of something big in racing, and he was ready to do battle on the circuit once again.

Gradually, Ray began to feel more comfortable in his role as owner, but along the way he learned that the job bears very little resemblance to his work experience up to this point. Once upon a time he could decide on the spur of the moment when and where to race next, sometimes driving all night after one race to get to another track and then sleeping in his truck in the parking lot. Today his schedule on the NASCAR Winston Cup circuit is laid out months in advance. On a typical week during the racing season Ray will fly back to Statesville, North Carolina, on the team plane after a race, usually arriving late on Sunday night. Early Monday morning he is in the Statesville office for two intensive days of meetings, planning, and paperwork, often interrupted on Tuesday mornings by a photo or video shoot. One of the team's sponsors may be producing a sales video or commercial, with Ray needed for some introductory spots. This means changing shirts once or twice, quickly reviewing a short script, and

Mercy is when you don't get punished when you know you deserve it. Grace is when you get something you feel you don't deserve. I always feel like I get a lot of grace and plenty of mercy.
—RAY EVERNHAM

Even though the ultimate victory can never be fully achieved, it must be pursued with all of one's might.
— VINCE LOMBARDI

HAVE *passion for your mission.*

sitting in front of the cameras while, behind him in the shop, the work goes on. He usually meets over lunch on Tuesday with his department heads.

Wednesday morning he goes to the engine shop in Concord, meeting with department heads there for three hours before perhaps boarding a plane for a speaking engagement on behalf of another sponsor, followed by a plant tour and a meeting with employees. Invariably, he records a few voice-overs to be used in radio ads. Late that afternoon he may fly back to Concord for yet another meeting at the engine shop; his day usually ends around seven, more than twelve hours after he arrived at work.

Thursday is departure day, and Evernham Motorsports is humming. The transporters have left, and Ray's clothing has been packed for the weekend with special attention to the appearances he'll be making and which sponsor shirts he'll need to wear. By late afternoon the team is on the plane en route to the next race. On arrival in the early evening, they climb into Dodges provided by the local dealership and head for dinner at their favorite local restaurant. After dinner the team heads for the hotel and Ray goes to

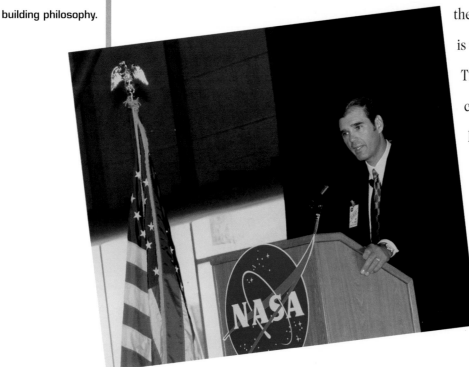

the race track infield, where his motor coach is waiting, and often Mary and Ray J as well. These weekends are the most time the family can spend together during the race season. Ray makes one nightly call to the local radio station, usually with a funny story about last week's race and a team update. Friday is qualifying day, filled with the sound and fury of racing engines and busy crews, and for the next three days Ray is on familiar ground—he is racing again.

*As long as I know I
have given 100 percent
every day, the ultimate
victory can't be that
far ahead of me.*
—RAY EVERNHAM

Ray Evernham's Twenty Points for Success

1. GOD AND FAMILY

Without God's grace and the support of my family, I would not be here now.

2. HARD WORK

It takes hard work to be successful. Life is not easy. It's not supposed to be.

3. DO WHATEVER IT TAKES

Any job that must be done, any position that must be filled to complete the mission, is your responsibility. Find a way.

4. SURROUND YOURSELF WITH GOOD PEOPLE

Look for overachievers. Learn to identify good people and figure out how to get them on your team. Learn what motivates them and provide that motivation.

5. SET THE WORK ETHIC EXAMPLE

Get in early and stay late. Work neatly and efficiently. Work in the same manner you expect your people to work.

6. ALWAYS PUSH TO GET BETTER

Do one thing every day that makes you a little better at your job. In our world, 75 percent is average. If you can get to 76 percent, you have three-fourths of your competition beat.

7. STUDY

To learn you must study. The world is full of books, videos, and information other people have gathered for years. Use it!

8. DON'T BE INTIMIDATED BY YOUR COMPETITION

Respect them, but don't let them intimidate you. Never underestimate your competition. Always try to overestimate them. If they are stronger than you think they are, you get beat. If they aren't as strong as you think, you beat them more easily.

9. BELIEVE IN THE TEAM AND THE PROJECT

Strong belief in a project by its leader trickles down to the troops. That belief soon becomes confidence.

10. BE WILLING TO PUT PERSONAL GAIN BEHIND THE PROJECT

When your mind-set changes from "What is this project going to do for me?" to "What more can I do to make this project successful?" you are about to accomplish big things.

11. MAKE CHANGE WHEN CHANGE IS NEEDED

Be willing to change direction when it is needed. Never change for the sake of change. Make sure you have a reason, purpose, and direction. Then make your change without looking back.

12. WORK ON YOUR WEAKNESSES

We all have them. Identify them. Go to work on them and eliminate them.

13. WORK ON COMMUNICATION

You can't lead if you can't communicate. Effective and clear communication is a great tool that is seldom used properly.

14. RESOURCES

Identify them, acquire them, and use them.

15. BE ABLE TO FOCUS ON SHORT-TERM GOALS WITHOUT DISTRACTION

You need long-range goals for sure, but you also need short-term goals. Train yourself to keep an eye on the tree while grabbing the low-hanging fruit first.

16. THE FREEDOM TO DO YOUR JOB

If you give someone a project, give him or her guidance, resources, and time frames, and let them go. Don't micromanage.

17. CREATE TEAM SPIRIT

Everyone wants to be part of something special. Create something special for your people to be a part of.

18. SHARE THE MONEY AND THE GLORY

Nothing great is ever accomplished alone. If money and glory reward your team's performance, make sure that everyone shares in the rewards.

19. ALWAYS HAVE A PLAN AND SHARE IT WITH THE TEAM

People have to know where you are going before they will follow you. Share your vision often, and soon your team will see it, too.

20. COMPASSION, PASSION, AND EMOTION

You can't be great without them. Have compassion for your people. Let them know it. Have passion for your mission. Make sure everyone knows it.

GOOD START

The Dodge crew's celebration at Daytona was the start of a long season of learning and success. Following spread: In the Food City 500 at Bristol, Bill Elliott (9) finished seventeenth while John Andretti's Dodge (43) took second on the short track.

*If you want to
win, you have to
have everything
mapped out.*
—RAY EVERNHAM

AFTERWORD

WHEN I LEFT HENDRICK MOTORSPORTS I was looking for a new challenge to rekindle the professional spark in me. This Dodge project has provided me with that and more, because it has been a true test—both personally and professionally. We had only five hundred days in which to put the program together. That meant building and testing the car, designing and constructing the engine, and then receiving NASCAR's approval of both. Once that was done, turning Evernham Motorsports into a competitive operation became the primary objective.

I have been blessed by all of the support I have received while facing this challenge. It's a fantastic feeling being surrounded by people who believe in me—my family, my friends, my team, and even the fans are great. People constantly look me in the eye and tell me they know that we're going to make it. That kind of support gives me the strength and the determination to continue even when I'm exhausted and frustrated. My team and their families show their unconditional support every day. There's no greater gift that a person can give than their time. My people give their time and effort unselfishly, and with that many people believing in this project, I know it's going to be successful.

The creation of Evernham Motorsports and my partnership with Dodge is not only the newest but also the biggest challenge of my racing career. It's been a tremendous ride for me in racing. I have been truly blessed. If it all ended tomorrow, I would have no regrets. The world would owe me nothing. However, I owe a great deal to numerous people—from Bob Weiss of Manalpan, New Jersey, who gave me my first chance to work on a race car, to Jim Julow, Lou Patane, Bob Wildberger, and all of my friends at Dodge, who put this program together and had the confidence in me to oversee it. There have been many others who have helped me. Some, such as Jeff Gordon, Rick Hendrick, and Jay Signore, are well known; but many are known only to me.

To my mom and dad, who have always put their children ahead of themselves; to my wife, Mary; my son, Ray J; and to all of my family members whom I have not spent enough time with; to all of the people who have believed in me; without you, I would not be where I am today and would not have had the courage to move forward. This life has been as much yours as it has been mine. There is a piece of you on every page. God bless and thank you. —RAY EVERNHAM

IN THE RUNNING
Bill Elliott (9) and Casey Atwood (19) put Dodge in the NASCAR mix with the Fords and Chevrolets for the first season since 1985.

Acknowledgments

The author wishes to thank the following people for their help: Ray and Mary Evernham, Jeff Gordon, Rick Hendrick, Jay and Barbara Signore, Ann Eaton of Evernham Motorsports, George Tiedeman, and Debby Robinson of Golin/Harris International.

The publishers would also like to thank the following people for their help and advice: Sara Bumgarner and Steve Fogerty of Evernham Motorsports, Patrick Mason of Golin/Harris International, David Kimble, Buz McKim of ISC Publications, Inc., and Dan Pinkham.

Leukemia is still the number one disease killer of children under the age of fifteen. To find out what you can do to help, contact one or both of the organizations listed below.
The Leukemia and Lymphoma Society
http://www.leukemia-lymphoma.org

1-800-955-4572
National Marrow Donors Association
http://www.marrow.org
1-800-745-2452

Photography Credits

©J. Lauren Photographers
66, 67

Cameras In Action, Inc.
89b, 96b, 100b, 101b, 104, 122, 144a, 144b, 149

Courtesy of Dodge Motorsports
136–137, 138–139

Courtesy of the Ray & Mary Evernham Collection
5, 16, 17, 18a, 18b, 19, 20–21, 22, 23c, 23b, 23a, 24b, 24a, 24–25, 25a, 25b, 26a, 26b, 27, 28–29, 30a, 30b, 31, 32–33, 34a, 34b, 37b, 38,

39, 40, 41a, 41b, 50, 51, 54a, 54b, 56–57, 58b, 59b, 59a, 60, 61a, 62–63, 62, 63, 64–65, 68, 74, 82–83, 93a, 107b, 110a, 113e, 116, 148a, 148a

George Tiedemann
6–7, 12, 14, 42, 43, 44, 46–47, 47, 48–49, 58a, 69, 70, 71, 73, 76–77, 81, 82b, 84–85, 87b, 88, 89a, 90, 93b, 96a, 97b, 100a, 101a, 102–103, 106b, 106a, 107a, 110b, 111, 112, 113a, 113b, 113c, 113d, 114–115, 117, 120–121, 124b, 124a, 125, 126, 130,

131b, 132–133, 135a, 141, 142–143, 148b, 154, 155

Gino Difilippo Jr.
35, 61b

Golin/Harris International
127b, 128a, 128b, 129a, 129c, 129b, 134

ISC Archives
52–53, 55, 72, 82a

Joe Robbins Photography
8–9, 10–11, 105b, 144–145, 152–153

David Allio
35–36, 36a, 36b, 36c, 37a

Nigel Kinrade Photography
45, 75, 78, 79, 80, 86, 87a, 94–95, 97a, 98–99, 105a, 108–109, 118–119, 123, 127a, 131a, 135b, 140b, 140a, 146–147, 150–151

Steve Baker/Highlight Productions
91, 92

Note: Letters refer to the position of the photo on the page, beginning from left to right and proceeding from top to bottom.